Don Hutchinson

BROKEN FAMILY

BROKEN FAMILY

PROMINENT
B O O K S
EDGE

5830 E 2nd St, Ste 7000 #9983
Casper, WY 82609
USA

Clipart designed by Freepik

DEDICATION

I dedicate my book to my brother, Kenny. May God rest his soul Kenny was a wonderful support to our mother, Janece, and me. Kenny did everything he could to try to help the family stay as family.

I dedicate my book also to my brother, Duane, and his wife, Paula, for always being there for Mom, Janece, and me. They, too, were always there and tried very hard to keep our family together as a whole.

I dedicate my book to Kenny's daughter, Diane, with her heavy heart tried so, so hard to help our family understand the need to support her father, Kenny, and their family through his illness. She was hurt so bad for her father's health but still tried to get the family to open their eyes to see that love and support to each other is more important than money.

To my ball-playing friends that brought youth and more fun into my life.

To American Airlines for the joy of a job all my life and continued travel privileges.

To Janece and my kids for supporting us and giving us joy as a healthy family.

Especially to my wife, Janece, who stood beside me our thirty-two years, so far. She believed in me, worked with me, traveled with me, and recorded all my games so I will be able to watch them when I am not able to run those bases anymore. And for her love for my mother to give her the special opportunity to live her senior winter years in a warm climate and a lovely place to live. She tried so hard to help my brothers and sisters realize that family was more important than money.

Proverbs 15:27 (Leadership Bible, New International Version):

"A greedy man brings trouble to his family,
but he who hates bribes will live."

WHAT I REMEMBER and from what I was told when I was a very small toddler, number 2 in birth order, one day Bill (my brother, 11 months older than I) was playing with me and pushed me into the pantry while I was in my baby bed. Bill crawled in with me, and if anyone recalls there was always flour, sugar, and lard on the counter; I am sure you can guess what I looked like after all containers were dumped in the baby bed. It took quite some time to clean up that mess from what Mom told me.

My brothers and I had to keep ourselves busy every day, even at a very early age. When we were still in diapers, Bill and I would head across a plowed field to go see Dad—this was a few hundred yards to the field next to the house. Needles to say, it did rain the night before. We did not get far before Dad saw us heading toward him. He stopped his field work to help us out. He took us by our suspenders, carried us to the house, put us on the porch, and called Mom, who was taking care of Pete and Marg as well as setting up for dinner when Bill and I just kind of slipped out to check on Dad.

As I recall, as we got old enough, we—Bill, Pete, and myself—had duties to do like Bill washed dishes, I dried, and Pete swept the floor Marg was too young to do duties yet, and before she reached helping age, she passed at age three from strep throat. We had a snowstorm at the time, and Mom and Dad could not get her to the doctor in time. A man from town plowed out to our farm to help us get her to the doctor, but she died in his arms before they could leave for the doctor (That man was the father of my wife now, which was fifty years after the incident.) Getting back to our duties, we helped Mom clear the table after meals. Dad would take his short nap. Our duties changed off and on, so we each did different things. On quite a few occasions, Bill would find an excuse to get out of his duties. You know, an upset stomach or something to get out of work After we got a TV, if there was time to watch *As the World Turns,* we did that. As we got old enough, we would go out and play a little ball before going back to work. Work was slopping hogs, feeding hogs, bailing hay, feeding chickens, milking cows, corn planting, plowing, and cultivating corn. I never saw Dad pick corn by hand, but I was told when you pick corn by hand, you have a basket on the side of the wagon where you put the best ear of com for seed for the next year. I recall they had a mesh on one hand to really go fast, ripping off ears and tossing them in the wagon.

Dad had three horses: Chuck Blackie, and Caption. My first job with Chuck and Blackie was to mow 20 acres of hay. I was a little afraid, being just ten or eleven years old, but Dad and Uncle Dean said all you have to do is say giddy-up and woooh, and when they wanted a bit of hay, just jerk the reins. They told me when I came to a corner, I just needed to pull to the right till I finish the field. Dad and Uncle Dean would be back by the time I would be done. And guess what? They were right. I got her done After a day or so, we raked the hay in rows and had a hay-picker-upper (was called a hay rake) that was pulled behind a hay rack. This picker-upper would pull the hay behind the hay rack on to two ropes called slings. When there was so much hay on a sling, they would stop, put two more slings on till the rack was full, making four-sling loads. We would then go to the barn and hook up to a pulley, which had a rope pulley tracker system, that would relay the bails from the hay rack up to hay' loft. I have to question the word "tracker"—I do not remember the correct name for that. The person that could stand the heat of summer would stack the hay in the hay mound. The person that was hooking the slings on the hay rack had a rope called the trip rope, which he would hold on to until it got to the point the stacker wanted the load dropped. The guy in the hay mound would holler, "Tripp it." The guy on the ground would pull the rope and say "Tripp it." That continued until the rack was empty and continued until the haying was done.

We were over to Grandpa's farm with Uncle Lee (who was a very slow in reacting) with a very short trip rope that did not go all the way to the back of the barn. Bill, about eleven or twelve years old, was driving the tractor to a certain spot in the yard to pull the hay rope with tractor to trip it into the hay mound and was daydreaming and missed the spot to stop until he heard his uncle hollering. He looked back and saw Uncle hanging to the trip rope on the side of the barn. Getting excited, Bill, got off the tractor and unhooked the rope and down came Uncle Lee! Don't recall him being hurt, but Uncle wouldn't say anything if he was run over by a train. He just kept working with us.

Speaking of putting hay in the barn, this farmer had a bull that he could not get to go in the truck. So they came up with the idea of putting a sling rope around the bull's belly and lifting him up like we did the hay. As the rope got tighter on the bull, the bull let out a big beller, and the horses that were pulling the rope were frightened and ran, which pulled the bull all the way into the hay mound. Needless to say they had to butcher the bull in the hay mound and take him down in pieces. A happening like that kept the bull from doing his job for the farmer.

Oats were another job for us boys! It seems like it was my job to drive the tractor (named Case LA). Dad had a rope rigged up on the tractor if I got in trouble, while he was sitting on the binder in the back, making the shocks. We were young at this time, about eleven, twelve, and thirteen. As we first started a field, we would go so the binder would go toward the fence. After round one, our second round, we would go the other way' so we no longer were running over the oaks. The binder had the rack on the left side that would hold about six bundles. We would go so far and get five to six bundles and dump them in rows alongside the rack until field was done. After the first round, I got a bad side ace and could not drive or stand up. Dad took me to the house. I curled up into a ball and rested. Dad had to replace me, so he got Pete, my younger brother of two years, to drive the tractor. I was hurting so bad, bur after about three hours, it went away. I went back to the field to see what was going on; Pete had challenges making his first round. He would turn the steering wheel and not turn it back so he would drive in the oats then figure out he had to turn the wheel back. Dad was feeling really good when he saw me coming back to drive again. I then had to straighten the rows my brother had messed up. After cutting it all, we would stack them into shocks, meaning stand them up on end so the oats would dry for a couple days. After the field was shocked and dried, it looked like a field of pyramids. We had to help our uncles do their oaks also. Shocking is a two-person job. We would help our uncles do the thrashing of their fields. This consisted of Grandpa, Uncle Sid, Uncle Jay and Uncle Dean. Grandpa Hutch had the thrash machine, an old La Case steel wheel that would pull the thrasher from farm to farm (about 2 miles per hour). Grandpa was always the straw stacker. By the end of the day, he was the black guy [covered with dirt]. We had a cream cooler that was hooked to the well that was full of pop and beer, so when the uncles went to field, it didn't take too long to fill their wagon and stop by the cooler—"beer time." When we finished one farm, we were off to another uncle's farm. Haying was the time women really put out a feast for dinner and supper for all of us workers. After everyone left the first day, we—Bill, myself, and Pete—were going to give them a head start for the next day, so we went out to the field, loaded up a rack, and worked our little fannies off. When our uncles came the next day we caught some slack—our load got moisture in it and the thrasher wouldn't work as easily as it does if it was dry. The oats that were thrashed were elevated up to a large bin in the corn crib, which was used to feed the chickens. A barrel was set by the hog pin. Each day it would be filled with skim milk, and after milking we topped it off with oats. Hogs would go nuts for that. I guess that mixture would ferment overnight to a hog's delight.

After supper it was time for chorus, which consisted of milking, slopping hogs, feeding chickens, gathering eggs, and pitching hay from hay mound to feed the cows. If we were not to worn out, we would play card with the light of a lantern. Never had to toss and turn in bed because we put in a full day. In the cold winter days and nights when we went to bed, it took a while to warm up my spot, but when I got it warmed up, I did not move because if I did it was very cold again. If the bathroom pressure would get to great, we would raise the window and get some relief out the window. Mother would say, "I told you kids not to pee out the window." We did not have a clue how she knew we did this relief thing. Well, it was not that hard to figure out when you saw the yellow streak down the side of the house.

When we could get away, we would go to the creek, which was a half mile west of our house. We built a log cabin and small dam to have a swimming pool Mom would say, "No swimming in the creek," so we would strip down to our shorts thinking we could get away with our swimming. Well, a week did not go by that Mom would say, "I told you not to swim in the creek!" We seemed to forget that our underwear would mm a little dark from the mud that was stirred up. When it came to doing laundry, Mom saw our undershorts and knew we were swimming in the creek again.

On another occasion while strolling down the creek bank, which was covered with tall cotton wood trees, I spotted a raccoon napping high on a branch. I called to our ventures bunch, brothers and friend, who were ready to stop our exploring or the great outdoors and go back to the house I told them I saw a raccoon up in the tree. They came running, thinking I said, "Where is the red crow?" "No, a raccoon is up there." So Bill, myself Pete, Ken, and neighbor decided we would catch this coon. The plan was for me to cut the branch off so the coon would fall to the ground, Ken was to knock him out with a club, and Bill was to put him in a gunny' sack. So neighbor and I crawled up the tree with a saw to cut off the branch. The coon was a little upset but stayed on the branch.

Neighbor held on to me while I sawed the branch. After I sawed nearly three-fourths the way through the branch, it began to fall. It hit on another branch, knocking the coon off the branch. It seemed like we were up a long ways. The coon came flying through the air. Ken was to knock out the coon, but when the coon came down, Ken went the other way. The coon hit the ground, staggered around, and went in a culvert, which was not that far away. We had to come up with another plan. We decided to put a sack on the other end of the culvert and smoke him out.

I do not know where we got the matches, but we gathered up leaves and tried to get them to burn, which didn't go well. The big brother of neighbor stopped to see what we were up to. He, of course, thought we looked like we needed his help. He got his gas can out and put a little gas on our leaves. That did the trick We waited and watched where we had the sack around the culvert. Soon enough, we heard little paws and in the sack he went. We carried him home, which was a half mile away. We put him in our rabbit cage to make a pet out of him or her. We went out the next morning, *gone*! He slipped out a little break in the wire. It sure made some good memories for us!

Thinking of creek experiences, I have more fun memories to share. One spring day, neighbor, Pete, and I were trying to float large chunks of snow down the creek What we would do is take a long pole and poke holes in the snow and try to pry it loose to float them down the creek. As we were doing this, we heard a "Help!" and looked around only to see a neighbor clinging to snow up to his neck We pulled him out and wanted to take him home, but he said his mother would put the hurt on him for getting wet. So we decided to build a fire so he could dry off. It took a while, but we did get him dried off. (Don't know where we got matches.) We never heard any more about that. We did try to pole vault across the creek; it never worked. The pole would always stick in the mud. Guess what happened to us! At another time, Bill, Pete, Joe, and myself were exploring for anything we could find. Water was high and very cold. Ken decided to check out the culvert where we caught the coon with the sack He crawled out to the end of the culvert to peek in; he slipped and fell into the cold water We pulled him out and made him walk home. We tried to get him to run to keep warm, but all he did was walk stiff-legged and bawled all the way home.

We looked forward to November every year. That meant pheasant season was opening. We were never very for from the house before we got our limited of three birds apiece. This was Mother's day for cleaning the birds. The family eat them fried, roasted, or any way they could be cooked the rest of the winter. On some occasions, Bill, who had a single-barrel 12-gauge shotgun, and I, with a single-barrel 410, would head for a fence row where a lot of pheasants would hide. As we went along the fence row, a bird would get up and Bill would not give him a chance The bird would be not less than 15 feet before a blast from Bill's 12-gauge would go off Needless to say, there was not much left of that bird. I would beg Bill to give me the first shot with my 410. I do not recall that ever happing. My next shot gun was a 20-gauge. My good friend John and I put a few miles hunting for the birds. We always got our share. One winter day, I and Pete decided to go hunting in a blizzard. We took off west along fence row; no birds, so we decided to go northwest up the creek—no birds. We stopped at our neighbor to warm up a bit. We were at least a mile and half from home. When we went outside to go home, we found the visit was great but the snow had melted in my boots. My feet got very cold, but we trudged on, shot a few birds, and stopped at another neighbor to get warmed up. Then off to Uncle Sid's, which was one mile east. Shot a few more birds on our way and gave them to Aunt E when we got there. Instead of calling home as we were leaving, which was one long and two shorts, we took off for home. We had a half mile southwest across the field to home. As we got halfway, Pete was wanting to lay down and go to sleep. I said, "Look, there is our house a few hundred yards ahead of us, as you can see." We made it home. We found out that Mom and Dad became concerned for us and were going to get an all-out search for us by our whole town. What would you think—blizzard, zero degrees, gone for over six hours? What would you do as a parent!?

Other hunting adventures: Buddy John, Mel, and I were cruising the countryside looking for anything, maybe a crow, chicken hawk, gopher, anything. Mel was cruising with his pickup in front of friend John. Mel spotted a hawk and slammed on his brakes; John was driving his rebuilt Lincoln Zephyr, which he had just overhauled and not gotten around to put a brake job on yet. Needless to say, we slammed into the back of Aid's pickup. You can guess John's words, "Ooooooh shiiiiiit." Mel had to push John to his home going on the back roads. Some farmer had his flock of birds (ducks, geese, chickens) on the road. Mel never slowed down. We found out why chickens should never cross roads!

It is a little different now in 2018; then, there were more wildlife in the fields than chickens in the chicken house. Jack rabbits, cotton tails, gophers, skunks, coons partridge, grouse, blackbirds, robins, and of course, sparrows plus many more. Few deer, fox, Canada geese. Of course, there were ducks going north and south. In our time, we never did too much duck or geese hunting. We gave the other birds a run for their money. Then the time came that ail the farmer took out nearly all fences and developed poison for any weeds that tried to invade their crops. Farming like this began taking all cover from wildlife and gave them no place to hide or take cover from winter snows. Needless to say, the bird population has become very small soon after that. Now, very seldom do we see a jack rabbit; no grouse, no partridge because they cut down all the pear trees. During winter we would shoot cotton tails and jack rabbits and hang them in the grove. When we got several, we would take them to Minnesota to a mink farm; cotton tails 10 cents, jack rabbits one dollar We would also trap the creek for musk rats, beaver, and coon. A good musk rat pelt would go for six dollars, beaver maybe twenty. I do not remember what coons went for. That was really a lot of work, up early to head to creek traps, pick up our bootie, reset our traps, and back home half mile away before school. Then after school we would skin our catch and hang them in the cellar to dry. There was always a person somewhere to purchase our furs that we worked so hard to get them ready for women to have the best fur coats in Iowa.

We did have to go to school, which was not my best thing to do. If it was not for baseball, I would not have gone very fir in school. We had to have some passing grades to play ball, so I had to buckle down to be able to play. I was not the best hitter in town, but I could really throw the ball where I wanted it to go. The last season of ball, I lost one game in high school and one game in junior league ball. My best throw was over a 320-foot fence in Bancroft, Iowa. Some folks still remember that. I think baseball was played any time we did not have anything to do. The corn crib door was nothing but a bunch of broken pieces of wood where the balls would hit it. Dad would pitch batting practice on occasion. Once in a while, he would rare back and fire one to us; needless to say, at our age we did not see the ball.

In 1947, Dad had a head-on wreck north of Algona, Iowa. My uncle, Joe, and Bud, were in the car with Dad. The person that hit him was driving an old model car. In those days the roads were not kept up. The other car slipped off the road and instead of slowing down and getting back on the road, he turned his steering, which came back into Dad's lane. This head-on crash messed up Dad pretty bad. Uncle was okay. Joe was standing up in the back seat and he flew toward the front and ended up with a big gash on his forehead. Bud was okay. We think Dad grabbed Uncle's arm to hold Bud from getting hurt. This all took place in the fall when it was corn-picking rime. All the farmers showed up at our form to harvest the corn. We had to get out of their way because the corn was picked before you could blink an eye Do you think that would happen today? (2018) (I want to believe so.)

Dad was not good after that. Later when I was working for Uncle, Dad came over to me to ask me if I could plant the corn for him. (I was in fourth or fifth grade. I don't know why he didn't ask Bill.) He just couldn't do it anymore because of the accident. That was my first time to plant corn. I did not do all that bad. At that time corn was checked, which means about three kernels per hill every 3 feet. The reason for that was because when they used horses, they were 3 feet wide. This was our way to cross-cultivate to combat weeds. A person did not daydream when cultivating or there would not be too much com to harvest.

Gophers would come along after planting corn and dig up our corn. We came up with a good throwing wrench to get rid of the gopher population. After com was planted, when we did not have anything to do, we would go gopher fishing. We had a rod and reel and a lasso made with the string. We would see a gopher go in his hole, put our lasso around the hole, step back, and wait for our gopher to stick his head out; a little jerk, bingo—one gopher. With the gophers in a sack, we would go up to our holding tank. I caught one Wesley. He was a mean little one. I had to hold him as far from me as I could so he did not take a chunk out of me.

Playing ball was my love. A few formers had a ball field on their place. Sundays we went to church and then figured out whose place was going to host all the ball players. In the forties and fifties was when my hometown, Lone Rock, had some of the best players in the state. They would show up to give the folks a show that no one would forget There was a black team that would tour the states to play for little or nothing. I saw Dad play against them. I don't remember if they won or lost. It did not matter. The whole country had some fun watching the games. Bancroft, Iowa, was 11 miles from us and where we went to church. Some of us went to school there. Bancroft put out two Major League players for the Dodgers and Braves. My brother, Pete, played Double AA for the Dodgers a couple years as short stop. I was in the army and came home on leave and Dad said, "Let's go to see Pete play ball in Ponca City, Oklahoma, 500 miles from our home." We packed up and headed for our ball game. I did the driving. On our way I would see a road sign curve and dip. I would slow up. After a few of those, it seemed to me that was a waste of paint. I slowed up a bunch of times and finally thought, well, no need to slow up, so I just kept the car on the speed limit. I found I should have paid attention to that sign. We hit the dip and went flying in the air. Luckily we hit the road a few yards down with a huge crunch. I stopped the car, got out, did an inspection; everything looked okay. I thought Dad was going to really give me the one- two but never did. After a full day's, drive we came to Ponca City. We got a hotel, checked in, and went to the ball park. Our weather was cloudy with a little fog. Dad said, "There will be no home runs today." Well, he was wrong. The first time Pete stepped up to the plate, *boom* over left field fence. The next year he had a "plus a ball" rating, whatever that was. In base ball we base regular ball and the better ball is a "plus ball" which is speed over 90 miles an hour. They wanted to get him to pitch because of how hard he could throw. So they had him throw a different way. He hurt his arm trying their way of throwing, so they let him go. He went home and went to college and got a job buying cattle.

I think just about all farm boys joined 4-H. Bill, Pete, and myself joined. Grandpa was a cattle feeder, so he had us go pick out our calves and take them home. We would feed them through the summer, getting them ready' for the county fair in Algona, Iowa. When they were auctioned off, we did well enough to buy our clothes and other stuff we needed for school, guns, shells, and a 1941 Ford for 200 bucks. I was fifteen at the time.

Brother Bill thought he was a racecar driver He would go down gravel roads like it was a race track. At times I would pull out the choke, which was located in the middle of the dash. That would flood the car and slow it down. We would go into hay fields and drive around looking for rabbits, pheasants, and whatever we could find. We had a field sparrow fly into the window of our car. We took him home and put it in our bird cage. Our canary had just died so we had space for another residence. After he settled down, maybe a couple of weeks, he started to sing. Then we though he needed a friend. So we caught a sparrow for roommate for him. He never sang another note. We took the sparrow out and that did not make any difference. He gave up on his singing.

On another dare: daredevil Bill, with our '41 Ford—of course, remember, Bill did all the driving because he was sixteen and I am 11 months younger—he was driving in a field with a bunch of bailed hay. Well, he decided to drive over one. It did not take too much to get hung up on that bail. It took us quite some time to dig that bail from under that car What it did was break the radiator drain plug off He drove the steaming hot car to the closest farm where the farmer cut a piece of wood and pounded it in the drain hole. That worked pretty good, but we still had to stop at nearly every farm to top off water I don't remember how it got fixed. Dad was the one that had the skill to fix nearly everything, except Bill.

Another time when we were supposed to go to church, we went out to pick a buddy up north of Bancroft to take him with us. On the way to church from his house, we were coming in from the east. There was a double curve that led us to Bancroft, Iowa. We headed into the first curve. Bill sorta slid around the first curve and did the same on the second. Bill said, "Let's get ready to give that another try." So back we went to do what was supposed to be a better run. We went through the first curve slinging gravel all over the place. As we headed into the curve, Bill put the pedal to the medal, sliding into the last curve, gravel flying, and the car slid off the road. The next thing we knew, we were slamming all around the inside of the car. We started rolling. We went wheel to wheel looking straight west into Bancroft, Iowa, as we landed. When we got settled down, the passenger door opened and my buddy fell out on the ground in a heap. Bill went berserk saying, "I killed him! I killed him!" I was so shocked. I ran into the cornfield, which is now Bancroft golf course. I mustered up some courage and went back out to the car. The lights were still on. I tried to turn them off with no luck. After a short while, other folks showed up. My buddy was taken to the doctor. When he came to, he did not remember even getting in our car to go to church. I had a scrape across the side of my head. I do not remember what Bill had. After all things settled down, we continued our after-church plans to go see *The Lone Ranger* at our local theater. In the movie, my leg started to hurt. Thinking back, that was why I could not turn off the headlights after our rollover. I had hit the switch with my leg. The next day we drove the car home. It looked like a *V.* The drivers side was bent down, and the passenger side was also bent down. It would still run so we drove it home with the right front wheel doing a very big wobble. I do not know if anyone got any chewing out for that. I think that incident taught Bill something. We parked it in the grove to work on it. We put a jack inside to try to push the inside back to where it was before the big rollover, it sorta worked. We replaced the wheel. It would go, but it didn't look like a Ford anymore going down the road. I think Dad did keep it around for a reminder of what reckless driving does to anyone.

After feeding cows all winter, we had an empty barn so we would tie ropes on the track at the top of the barn. After we had the ropes set up, we could swing from one end to other. The "city boys from Lone Rock" would come our and play all kinds of games. We would tie one bale with one rope, another rope on another bale, and swing toward each other trying to knock one of us off. There was hay on the floor so no one got hurt. When we got tired of that, we got our ball stuff and played ball. We always found ways to have fun and keep ourselves busy growing up.

Not for sure what year it was, but early one morning Dad hollered upstairs. "The barn is on fire." We looked out our window, which was facing the west toward the barn. All we could see was rafters because the shingles had burned off. Dad ran into the front of the burning barn. He had to get all the cows out and got part of the cream separator, which has flowers planted in it to this day in front of the house Mom lived in Lone Rock, Iowa. There was no need for a firetruck because it burned so fast. It was too far gone by the time they got there. The corn crib was next to the bam so the firefighter watched that very carefully so it didn't start burning. The barn smoldered for several days. When all settled down,

Dad had a bulldozer guy from Lone Rock come out and bury the remains of what was left of our "fun" and "work" place. The fire was started by lightning. We never had lighting rods on any building, but after that all the farmers installed lighting rods on their tall buildings. Other barns burned down. Our neighbor's burned because he had put up a bunch of wet hay, which overheated and caught fire The other barn and machine shed was Uncle Sid's. His kids set a little fire in the buildings, which got out of hand.

I never had to go without a job. One winter there was an ice storm that covered all the telephone fines. Our Lone Rock telephone man called Dad to see if his kids were busy. With all the ice that covered everything, we had nothing to do except our chorus. Dad volunteered me to help him. I do not know why only me. He came and got me, gave me a long pole, and said, "Go to the middle of every telephone pole. Hit the wire as hard as you could." You can just see how long the pole had to be. I put the pole between my legs, pulled up as hard as I could, and it worked. It was very cold that day, but after the first couple of poles, I warmed up, so I was okay. That was kind of rewarding to see the ice fall to the top of the icy snow making a straight line from pole to pole. After a few miles the telephone man came, picked me up, and went to places where telephone lines were broken. We repaired broken lines till dark. The next day we started over until we finished our work.

I got another job with a neighbor He had a Case bailer and needed help doing family-farm baling. I was glad to have the job of driving his tractor I can't remember the name of his tractor I received a penny per bale. On a good day, I could make ten dollars. The bailer was not an automatic baler He was the needier, which consisted of a double bar where a person would shove two bale wires, one on top, one on bottom, to the tier setting in the worst place of baling. A lot of farmers would work together when pitting up bailed hay. They would have maybe three hay wagons to shuffle the wagons from the barn to the bailers. We would take a full rack of hay bales to the barn and put an empty one behind the bailer to be loaded. I think, if I remember correctly, we had around sixty bails per rack, more or less. On a good day we could maybe bale one thousand bales. At a penny a bale, that was a good day.

Some farmer wives would bring us a midday snack for our midday break. That was good also.

My Uncle Dean ran Grandpa's firm after he retired to Bancroft, Iowa. I believe Uncle was chosen because he was the only son that didn't marry. Grandpa's home was in Bancroft, just across from St. John's Catholic Church. We enjoyed stopped in for a while to visit after mass every Sunday. We saw all our cousins there also. And there were a lot of us. The house usually was full. Most of my cousins were "big" families like ours. You know, good Catholic families!! Grandpa, so often, would stand out front enjoying picture taking with all of us.

I worked for Uncle Dean one summer. During that summer I learned how to spread manure. "Never, never, start the spreader downwind, especially when the wind is blowing hard downwind!" Needless to say, it did not take me long to turn off the spreader. I was a little embarrassed when I pulled in the yard to load up for another trip to go back to the field. On my second trip out, I made sure I was facing the wind before I turned on the spreader. I did not have to do that a second time to learn the wind in my face was important when spreading manure!

Uncle Dean always had his international tractor going full blast in a low gear, no matter whatever he was doing. When he would plow, if he could, he would plow two feet deep. He had me mowing hay, downhill, on a very windy day, which would blow the hay in front of the mower, yes, plugging up the mower I would get off the tractor, unplug the mower, and start mowing again. After going through that same thing over and over, I saw Uncle Dean leave. When he got out of sight, I shifted the tractor up to a higher speed. I was going to get something done. At a faster speed the mower would not plug up. Uncle Dean came back and caught me and chewed me out so I had to poke along doing the same thing, plugging the mower, until he left again.

Uncle Dean and I would trade out weekends feeding cattle. When I would feed cattle, I always have my 222 rifle setting where I could get ahold of it in case a pigeon would stick his head above the top of the barn where I could shoot his head off. After shooting a few, I would take them to Uncle Dean's hired man's wife and she would fix a meal for us. The place was covered with pigeons, rats, and mice. Every day I put out rat poison. When I quit and went to the army, there were very few rats and mice left. That summer Uncle Dean and I were baling hay. I was on the hay rack stacking hay when I saw out of the corner of my *eye* something—didn't really pay a lot of attention to it. The next thing I knew, a bumblebee hit me right between my eyes as I was lifting a bale to place it on the rack Shortly after the bee hit me, we got the rack full and headed back toward the house one-half mile away. By the time we got there, I could barely see. Uncle Dean took me to the doctor in Bancroft. The doctor said, "You are very lucky—if you were stung any more, you would have to get a gravestone." He just said, "Go home, wait for the swelling to go down, and go about your business and stay away from the bees."

One other time Grandpa, Uncle Dean, Dad, and myself were plowing a picked cornfield. I had a DC Case with hydraulics hooked to my plow, so when the corn would start to plug up, I would make adjustments to my three-bottom plows. That way I could eliminate plugging up my plow. Grandpa had a two-bottom plow that would plug up quite a bit. He must have noticed I was not plugging up that day. We took a dinner break Grandpa hurried up, chowed down, and went out and gassed up my tractor He then headed for the field with my tractor to plow as much as I did that morning. He only made the mistake of not looking back to see how things were going. His plow was so plugged up, the tractor could not pull the plow; he only made one round that day. Oh, say he did come over one day after that to help Dad plow the north field. I guess he got to daydreaming and forgot to trip the plow. When you don't raise the plow, it is very hard to turn the tractor He just plowed right through the fence and made a big turn in the field next to the one he was plowing. It was a wonder he didn't tear up the whole fence. After the fence came loose, he just went back to the field and finished his plowing. That was in his later years. Grandpa was a good old guy. Too bad all folks were not like him!

Another memory I remember is Grandpa and Uncle Lee painting a large shed. Grandpa said, "I just don't understand how you keep going all day long and not get tired." Grandpa was getting too old to farm, middle eighties. As I think back after he moved to town, he enjoyed sitting in his lounge chair and reading the paper.

Uncle Dean farmed the land until he had to go into the Bancroft nursing home. He was found in the bathtub one day in his farmhouse by Bill. He had gotten in to take a bath and could not get out. From what I remember, he had been there three days. Uncle Dean then rented the farm out until his passing. Uncle Dean lived several years before he passed. From what I understand, he gave the staff at the nursing home a lot of challenges his last days. Everyone said he was a jerk and thought only of himself. I tilled to share earlier, before Uncle Dean took over the firm, he traveled the world. When Uncle Dean died, he surprised us forty-three nieces and nephews in his will by willing each of us around ten thousand dollars. Well, goes to show you, we don't really know some people! Later in my book I will go more into that.

Early farmers were known for raising pigs in those days. With pigs, we also had a time to castrate the little ones. Some of my uncles would get together and go from firm to farm to castrate the little pigs. After the castration was finished, Aunt E would deep fry the "nuts," which were called "mountain oysters," for all of us. They are not much different than the regular oysters. We also had a feast of oyster soup when the harvest was over, at Uncle Sid and Aunt E's. She was a very good cook. That would dose out our year of harvest.

I will tell you what I remember about Lone Rock, Iowa. Driving in from the south looking to the east, the first thing you would see was the auction barn, which stayed very' busy. Next was a lumberyard, which was made into a bar in later years. Across the street was a grocery store, which had a butcher shop in the back; it did a great business. There was an apartment above the store. Just east of the grocery store was a blacksmith shop. Just north of the grocery store was a barbershop, which never did a great deal of business. That was also a two-story; if I remember, the top floor was an apartment Next to that was a bar and pool hall. When we were hungry for ice cream, that's where we would go. For a nickel or maybe it was dime, we could get a scoop of ice cream; that was huge. John, my best friend, and I learned to play pool there, which was in the back I think it was ten cents per game.

Above the pool hall was the Lone Rock Hall, where meetings were held and free movies. The town folks would put on a free movie every Saturday night. If the weather was nice, they would have an outdoor movie behind the bank which was located just north of the cafe. A lady and her daughters from town would bring up her popcorn machine and sold bags of popcorn for five cents a bag. The little cafe really did a booming business also. Next to that was the post office and a little bank. Just south of that was our Chevy dealer. They had a Coke machine: five cents for a Coke, one cent for some peanuts; put the peanuts in the Coke, a great little snack For six cents, what more could you ask for? In the alleyway behind the bank was the Lone Rock Jail It was about a ten-by-twelve room. Never did know if anyone was ever thrown in that jail. It should still be there, and used, for what some folks have done. On the northwest end of town was the church. Back up on Main Street across the street was a creamery, which did the whole yard—milk, cream, butter, cottage cheese, and regular cheese If it could be done, they could do it. Just south was the telephone company, with the old board that had a bunch of holes in it. When someone called in to the operator to talk to someone, the operator would pull a wire from another board and plug it in a hole, which the operator knew connected to the party they wanted. The operators knew everything that was going on in the whole country. The lines were hooked up in sections. When one was called, everyone in that section knew who was being called. There were a few that would quietly pick up their phone to what they called "rubbernecking." That way they could keep up with all the goings-on in the community'. Just north of that was an implement dealer, which did not last that long. They tried building trailer homes. I don't know how long that lasted. The telephone phased out, and so did the trailer building venture. It was torn down, and a new bank was built That bank lasted for years because it was a family-owned bank. It then was sold to a bigger bank. Next the post office, then another grocery store, and just south of that was the lumberyard office and store. South of that across the street is and still is the Lone Rock Coop elevator. We had three businesses that sold gas at that time. The lumberyard, grocery store, and car dealer Southwest of town was the railroad station, which is still there.

It is now full of community history. That train hauled everything from passengers to firecrackers. A person could see and hear the train coming from miles away. A whistle that could be heard, and a cloud of coal smoke seen for miles. There was a group of people called "hoboes' that would get on the train anywhere they could; mostly they would ride the empty box cars and go begging from town to town. Uncle Gee must have had a sign on the track, because nearly all the tramps would stop for a free lunch. Their place was just a couple hundred yards north of the track.

Now just west of the train station, a historical country church was hauled in from the countryside Just west of the church is "The Lone Rock" Rock, which the town's name came from. It was hauled in from a field located about two miles north of town. Years ago I suggested the rock be moved to town because Lone Rock was named after that rock Town folks said there is no machine big enough to move that rock. After a few years, they found the equipment to move that rock by breaking it into three pieces. The original town was built by that rock way back when. I do not know for sure what year that was. When the railroad came through, which went from Fenton, Iowa, to Burt, Iowa, missing Lone by a mile and a half they just moved Lone Rock to the track in 1970.

"In the early days, a large, lone boulder lay nestled in the prairie grass on a farmstead one and half miles north and one and a half miles east of the present town of Lone Rock."

Before roads were established, this boulder was used as a landmark from Fort Dodge through Armstrong and Estherville, to Spirit Lake.

A tiny settlement consisting of a store, creamery, post office, and a house sprang up near the rock *A farmwife nearby named the settlement "Lone Rock."*

In 1889, the Chicago and Northwestern Railroad Company built a branch line from Burt to Fox Lake, *Minnesota. It seemed only reasonable for the small community to move to the railway. The town so moved and kept its name.*

In 1970, the town of Lone Rock formed a *development corporation. These people took on a 175-ton project of moving the "rock" to town.*

There were several problems involved. *The rock was half buried, and no machinery was available to move the huge rock of 10' x 12' x 10' high. It teas necessary to blast the rock into four pieces. Then came the procedure of moving it to the southwest comer of town and then putting it back together again, as close as possible to its original form. Mission accomplished!*

The historical society has taken on the task of renovating the depot that had been used by the Lone Rock Cooperative Elevator for some *time since the railroad disbanded in 1974. The depot was built some time prior to 1900 and had been rebuilt in 1950. We now hate a Lone Rock Museum in this depot and many of the original artifacts of the area are on display, one of these being a telegraph key Also a baggage cart and a hand cart from the era."*

In July of 1999, *Lone Rock celebrated their 100th birthday!*

I was told the "Rock" was where the generals and their troops would meet to discuss how they were going to track down the Indians to rid them from Iowa. The rock was located one mile straight east of our farm, which, on several occasions, Bill, Pete, and myself reenacted the stories we heard. We did have a great imagination!

Getting back to Lone Rock On the northwest end of town was a two-story building called the Lone Rock School Two stories, grade one and two in one room; three and four in other room located on the ground floor. The basement was located under first, second, third, and fourth grades. In the basement was the furnace and shop for woodworking and such. Lower floor on the south was the gym. Top floor to the north was grade five and six; in the other was seven and eight. When you were in grade eight, you were looking forward to going across the hall to high school.

All grades were in one room, one line per grade. There were two rooms for classes on the cast side. When it was our turn to have our classes, the others would move out. Onc class in and one class out The class I liked best was P.E., which was determined by what time of year it was. Winter—basketball and just because my friends and I were too short to play basketball, we played ping-pong. We got pretty good at that When it was getting close to spring, we used the gym to play catch, for baseball. We were getting our arms in shape to go to the ball park Lone Rock had one of the best teams in Iowa. For a town of one hundred fifty population, we held our own! Lone Rock had two families with trucking business, one was located across the street from the school. The other just a block away across the street. Out north of town there was a chicken hatchery. The person that owned that hatchery was called "Happy Cotton." At times when we walked home from school, he would have us in for ice cream. Good folks. Talk about walking home. I remember riding to school on ponies, which didn't go over well with me. I would double with our neighbor. The ponies we had seemed to bounce so bad, I would get such a bad side ace. My neighbor had to slow down. Needless to say, we were late for school at times. Lone Rock had a stable located just northeast of the school. We were one of the few kids to ride ponies to school.

Bill was a pretty good pony person. On one occasion the Shetland pony he was riding tried to brush him off by going along a fence. Bill was brushed off and ended up with a big cut in his leg. That kind of put the fear in me Our pony-riding group said, "Okay, it is your time to ride by yourself to school." I did not hurry that pony because he was the one that put the cut on Bill's leg. We stopped by the neighbors. He wanted to cut me a stick so I could hurry the pony along a little fasten we were only two hours late to walk a horse two miles. Now that I think about that situation, a person would think that I could be relieved from my pony. Pete and two neighbors wanted to blame me for being late and enjoyed every minute of it. I just could not get along with any horse.

One of my first duties was to water the pony that was in the barn. I started leading the pony out the barn door, which had an eight-by-eight plank that I had to step over. Well, the pony was in more of a hurry than me. It knocked me over that plank, stepped on my chest and belly, and went out and got his own water. He didn't need me to water him. Another time, Pete and I were racing back to the house to where Dad was doing fieldwork. We were really going top speed. When we came to a gate that was closed, our ponies came to a sliding halt And of course, Pete did just what all the cowboys did with their horses. I did not have all that experience. My pony stopped. I did not. I went flying right into the gate. I don't remember breaking anything—just my pride—which, at that time, I did not know what pride was. Later that year we had a family outing on our farm. Pete and I were down the lane going to race to the house where there was a lot of family gathered. I was a little afraid because the ponies had a habit of running into the bam. I felt real good about myself, got the pony stopped, sitting in the saddle thinking I did good, when I found myself head first in our gravel yard. What happened was Uncle Dean was going to hop on back of my pony. The pony was not aware of what was going on. My pony gave a huge kick, throwing me off the front over his head. It took some time, but they got all the gravel out of me. Uncle Dean was going to give me a dime for all the bumps that I received from my fall; needless to say, "no dimes."

I was part owner of that '41 Ford—you know, the one Bill rolled just east of Bancroft. It was my first car. My next one was '47 Kaiser. This was the car Dad bought after he had that head-on crash north of Algona. Pete was driving the Kaiser coming back from Bancroft when he met a car. They both were taking their side out of the middle of the road and sideswiped each other, tearing up the driver's side front fender. Seems that after that, no one wanted anything to do with that Kaiser. I noticed a '47 Kaiser in a grove that the motor was blown, so I had it towed to our house. Dad and I took the engine out of our '47 and put it in the other. To me I had a class-act car. I could get it up to sixty if I were heading downhill. It would get me where I wanted to go. For a high-school project, I decided to paint my car. We, meaning our "class," sanded and prepped for painting. I went to Algona to the paint store, told him what I was doing, and what he would recommend. He said, "What color do you want?" I told him two different color greens—one light, one dark. He mixed the paint for me to take back to my, "our," project.

We decided to paint the trunk and hood dark green. We drew a line from the front wheel to the back wheel and painted the lower part dark green. The rest of the car was light green, sharp. If you should ask around Lone Rock, some folks still remember that car.

I drove that car to South Dakota to buy firecrackers so we could have fireworks for the Fourth of July. When I came back through a small town in Iowa, I had to stop for gas. When I pulled in the gas station, they said, "We saw you go through town this morning." I questioned them and said, "Are you sure it was me?" He said, "Yes, that is the only car in the country that looks like that."

I had our fireworks on the Fourth. The family invited all the cousins to watch my fireworks. It was going real well until I got some help from [I don't remember who]. He lit a sparkler too close to the box that had all the fireworks. Guess what, my' fireworks was over in just a few minutes. Everyone went running for cover! That was the last time for me to have a fireworks outing.

I just cannot recall what happened to my '47 Kaiser. My next car was a 1954 Henry J. I had worked enough to put a down payment, and with the help of Dad, I drove home in a brand-new '54 Henry J., which was red to me. If I remember right, Dad and I did all this when we went to see Mom, who was in the hospital with a newborn baby boy, giving our family seven boys. That car was my go-to-school or work car and even my date car.

I do not recall how I met a little girl from Fenton whom I dated. We did a lot together—movies, ice fishing, picking apples at Uncle Dean's. I would crawl up the tree and toss apples to her. Sometimes I would toss two at a time. She never missed. She spent a lot of time at our farm helping us do dishes and so forth. One time when she was washing dishes, little brothers would take the washed dishes from where she put them over to where they were to be washed. After a while, she caught on. All had a good laugh. At that time mixed marriage was a no-no in my family of faith. That kind of bothered me, so I joined the army, only to find out later in life, mixed marriage only meant to me someone with different beliefs. When I went to the army, I let Dad trade in my Henry J. along with Dad's car and he bought a new 1956 Chev. I didn't have my Henry J. paid for, so with my seventy dollars from the army a month, I would send 30 bucks a month until Dad said, "Okay, you are paid up."

I spent two years in the army. I was located in New Jersey in a "Nikie" base. My job was to run radar to protect the United States from illegal aircraft that may be out to bomb the US. To make extra bucks, I would do another guy's personal duties and man radar for them. I became real busy during payday because there was a bunch of guys that played cards and did a lot of gambling. The ones that lost their paycheck would come to me and give me two for one until their next paycheck.

I also got a job working in the PX that was located on the base. I just sold beer, pop, toothpaste, cigarettes, candy bars, and other stuff. The last year I got in the motor pool, which I drove to Fort Dix, to pick up rations for the other bases, which there were three. When our company had baseball games out of town, I drove our company bus to the games. We played several games in Philadelphia Pen. We ended up in Bel Air, Maryland, playing a bigtime tournament. I was hitting so well before going to Bel Air, the coach put me in clean-up spot. Did not do worth for the team. Darn.

The first part of November, buddies and I took a trip to New York We went sightseeing through just about all of New York We took a boat ride out to the Stature of Liberty. I do not know how many steps that were all the way to the top—a bunch. We looked out the statue s head and saw New York and, of course, the ocean. On the way down, I was getting very tired. When I got to the bottom, I just collapsed right down to the floor.

My legs could hardly hold me up. The guys took care of me. They got me back to the base. The next morning I had ration run. That meant I had to drive to Fort Dix to pick up rations. When I got to Fort Dix, my first stop was to pick up fruit. The guys that were there said, "You do not look very good." I was just about to pass out when they took me to the hospital. They dropped me off and put me in the waiting room where I stayed for hours. After a while someone took my vitals. Must not have been very good because they put me to bed. I stayed in bed for three days—no food or drink. Lying there, I heard someone say, "The person in that bed has not moved for three days. Maybe we need to check him out." They got me out of bed and sent me to an ears, nose, and throat doctor. He looked me over, gave me a shot, and put me back to bed. The next day it was like I was never sick I was supposed to get out of the army on November 15. Because of my being sick they had to do all the paperwork over.

I forgot to mention that I bought a '47 Mercury. My buddy would drive it to go Atlantic City every weekend when we were not on duty. Needless to say there were lots of pretty girls on the beach. I did meet a preacher's daughter from Bel Air, Maryland. We had a good time, but it did not go very far. We would go to the Steel Pier to a few shows. We found a cafe that served ice cream. I really enjoyed ice cream in every way possible. I got to know the person that dished up ice cream. I said, "Why don't you put two scoops in a dish with two cherries on top and call it a Marilyn Monroe?" They did, and every time I went in there, I got all the Marilyn Monroes I wanted. That went over big for their business! When I finally got my papers to go home, I loaded my car, which was not much. This was in December so when I went through the hills in Philadelphia, Pennsylvania, all of a sudden I started to slide down the road sideways. Needless to say, when I rolled to a stop, the next bunch of miles I drove very slow. When I finally got to Chicago, I knew I was getting close to home. That gave me my second breath. I cruised into Algona about seven hours later, then finally Lone Rock This was a start of a new time in my life. I have served my country and enjoyed seeing how others lived in cities.

After I got home, I had a relapse from my stay in the hospital in New Jersey. So back to the doctor and he looked at my tonsils and told me to come back in about two weeks; that should give the tonsils time for the swelling to go down. Dad brought me back to the Emmetsburg, Iowa, hospital in two weeks. The hospital staff did their thing, put me in one of green backward nightgowns, wheeled me down a hall, and gave me a shot in the arm. "See you later," they said. Next thing I remember was waking up to see Dad and the doctor The doctor said, "I should not have done that operation because your tonsils were as large as golf balls." Then he said, "Do you want to see them?" Of course I did. He handed me a jar, and I tried looking through the glass. I couldn't see very well, so

I took the lid off to see. When I got a whiff of whatever my tonsils were stored in, I nearly lost it Doc said, "Go back to sleep so you can rest up to go home tomorrow." I got up early the next morning and paced the lobby floor for a couple hours while waiting for Dad and the hospital to release me. After a while all things got taken care of.

Next day, Mom had a project. They were stripping all the wallpaper of the kitchen ceiling and walls. Seems like I was the only one to help with this project We had hot water that we would rub on the paper to loosen it up.

I was okay with the walls, but when it came to the celling, that was a different story. I had to put my head back, which made my neck bleed. When my mouth would fill up with blood, I would go outside, spit out blood, go back, and go to again. Nobody seemed to be concerned about me. I guess it was okay because I didn't feel all that bad.

Thinking about all these incidents, one day when I was younger, Bill and I went out to a cattle lane that led to the north fields. This lane had grown up with real tall weeds. We decided to get a corn knife; one for me and one for him. We were going along really good until I came across a large weed. I called to Bill to take a look at this weed. I was chopping away at the weed when Bill said, "Let me help you." Next thing I knew I had blood running all over the place. I started bawling. Bill said, "Don't cry, don't cry." Well, I did not feel like it hurt, so I stopped crying. Can you just think about what Mom thought when she saw me come in the house covered with blood? Dad—seems like it was always Dad—carried me to the doctor in Fenton, Iowa. He just cleaned me up and shaved my head where the cut was. Four or five medal clamps later, we went back to the farm like nothing happened.

Another time I picked a piece of board. For no reason, I threw the board. It had a nail in it. Guess what? I ripped a big hole in my right finger That was no big deal. It just got better after a couple of weeks. Another rime I was helping our hired man cut potatoes in half for planting. In our cellar we had a tater bin that would hold a pickup load of taters. The hired man and I were going through the tater, sorting for cutting in half for spring planning. I was very careful at first. After cutting a bushel or so, I held up my tater and with a swing of my knife, bingo, two pieces of taters. That was real good, so I called to the hired man and said, "Look at this," and gave a swing at my tater. That was all I did for that day. I had cut my thumb nail off. I went upstairs. Mom wrapped it up, and I just went on my way for the day. I did get out of washing dishes until it healed.

Another time in high school during shop, Aunt E wanted a picket fence made out of snow fence boards. As a lot of people know, that wood is really rough. I was putting the wood through a plainer to make them smooth. I was using a tool to hold the wood so it would plain the wood smooth. That wasn't working all that well, so I started doing it by hand. It didn't take me long to know why you need to use another piece of something to push the wood a person is working on. The piece I was working on broke getting my two middle fingers on my right, just about cut badly. When it happened, I said, "There goes my baseball." That really messed my spring up for baseball All I could do was go around with my right hand messed up and could not do a whole lot of anything with my right hand. The teams we played thought that was just okay, They didn't have to face me pitching that spring.

It was a different story that fall after my fingers healed. Most guys from other schools knew my reputation in pitching. (A lot of the players that I played have passed away now.)

After getting home from the army, I spent the winter of 1957 helping a feed grinder with his business. In the spring of 1958 I went to Kansas City. Dad had seen an ad in some paper that Weaver Airline School was advertising for people to learn the general workings for the airline business. I contracted them, and they told me they had classes starting in April and still have a few openings. So I headed that way in April to learn the airline business. There were three other guys from Iowa.

After a couple of days of school, we decided to have a party. I picked up a gallon, or maybe it was a half gallon of Mogen David wine. To me it was like drinking grape juice. I never was a drinker even in the army. As the night went on, I found out there was a huge difference between that and grape juice. I was not able to get back to my room that I rented for two weeks. My friends had to carry me up to bed. The only way I made it through the next day was to drink a Coke on every break we had. Just after a few days, the school got a call from New York and Chicago asking for all the young boys from Iowa, and they could have a job as soon as they could get there. Four of us gathered up our things and headed for home. I packed my things for my future in Chicago with American Airlines. On my own, like always, I took off for Chicago. I don't remember any family tears being shed when I left. I headed down Hwy 169 to Hwy 20 on my way to Chicago for my second job in the big world. Of course the army was my first job. I didn't travel with maps. I just stopped and ask for directions and watched the sky to find out where the airport was located after I got closer to Chicago. I had to stop on occasion to check out the sky to get my directions. On arrival I checked in to a short class for only a few hours. They told me to show up in the morning for work I never asked how much per hour I was going to get. I found out later it was one dollar and seventy-five cents per hour. That sounded real good to me; any extra time was time and one-half; never did get too much of that. I got a room not too far from work so I could walk to work. At that time I could walk on the airport grounds without anyone running me off. After a couple of paychecks, I bought a much-needed newer can My old '47 Merk was on its last leg. One of my buddies took me car shopping. I looked at a Studebaker. I talked over a price. It was a little more than what I wanted to pay. So he showed me a 1954 Ford. The salesman told me, "I just got a real good deal." After giving him fifteen hundred dollars, I left with a 1954 two- door, six-cylinder Ford, low mileage. I got a deal of a lifetime. He was right: 1 and that car went many miles together. I drove her on Lake Shore Drive many times, which was at that time one of the "drives" in the city of Chicago. I felt good also when I had my dates—the few dates I had!

My workday at Midway Airport with American Airlines was a piece of cake. I worked on DC 6 or DC 7 or maybe a small two-engine airplane. Our team had jobs. Belly man—his job was to unload the bellies of our planes that were assigned to our gate. Mailman—before the flight came in, he would go to the post office to pick up the airmail (I don't think there is any more air mail—it's just mail). He picked up mail from our flight, loaded the outbound mail, and went back to the post office to turn in his inbound mail. Then there was a person to do the freight, which was on the other side of the field that was over a mile away. He did a lot of time in his tug (tractor), which was orange back in 1958. Our bag runner delivered all the bags to their final destination.

Each crew had a crew chief that took care of the paperwork plus helped where help was needed. When we finished the ground work, we went up to the cabin to see if the stewardess needed any cabin service work. I don't know if they were prettier back then or it was just me. I think they had to be a certain size, etc., in those days before they were hired. All the airports only had ramps that were pushed to the plane by hand. That way we got to see all the bigshots, movie stars and so on. When the plane came to the gate, it was like a wedding—everyone was hugging and kissing. When they were boarding, it was like a funeral—everyone was sad and crying.

Nineteen fifty-eight was also the year *North by Northwest* with Carey Grant was filmed at Midway Airport. I got to see all the celebrities because they walked through the ramp I worked to the terminal for their filming.

One day when I was working the ramp, a parakeet landed on a piece of equipment. I walked over and grabbed him. It bit me a couple times. I just put him in my lunch bucket and took him to my apartment. I went to a pet store and bought a bird cage and some bird feed. He kept me company for a while until I transferred to Dallas, Texas. I gave him away to one of my neighbors.

I received a free trip on a 707 for Mom and Dad to go to Disney World in California. Dad and Mom came into Chicago to meet up with me. My buddy took us to O'Hare airport. O'Hare had just opened for the larger planes. When I checked us in, I did not have a trouble getting us in first class. Mom and Dad had never experienced anything like that before. Our flight went just south of Des Moines, Iowa, which had a huge thunderhead hovering over downtown. It was interesting to see. We had a good flight. We got a hotel close to Disney World in California. We had a wonderful time, especially riding bumper cars. I can still see Mom and Dad's expressions on their faces as they raced around that track One evening after a full day at Disney World, we went back to our hotel. At our hotel was a young lady standing outside the door. She looked at me and said, "Come on. I think you will do." Now that was right in front of Mom and Dad. They caught on way before I did! My first thought was, "What will do?" I guess she was trying to pick me up.

The next day we went to visit someone that used to work for Uncle Dean. We spent the day with them. The next day we flew to Phoenix to visit some retired Lone Rocker friends. At that time Phoenix Airport only had three gates for all airlines and everyone picked up their luggage outside on the luggage rack.

Flying back to O'Hare field in Chicago, I knew Mom and Dad had an experience of a lifetime. I was glad that American Airlines gave us that privilege.

I worked for American Airlines for one year in Chicago, then transferred to Love Field in Dallas, Texas. I left Chicago with my two-tone green and white 1954 Ford, parakeet, and very few clothes. The people I worked with were a great group of people. I enjoyed that year in Chicago and smile at the fun I had. I went on my adventure with a full head of hair and a goatee. I knew I could just trim my hair myself, but as I tried to trim it, things got out of hand. I ended up having to shave my head and face. I was trying to save money because my one dollar and seventy-five cents an hour was not getting me rich.

I left for Dallas, Texas, after getting all packed up, went out of town on highway 80 going west. I had a few days so I went home to Lone Rock, Iowa, to visit Mom and Dad. After a few days with family—which at that time I thought was the best in the world because Dad was in charge—I had to leave for my new location: Dallas, Texas.

I packed up my parakeet and headed south. Interstate 35 was being worked on at that time, not ready for travel. I stopped at the Red River for a couple photos and a break. When I got tired, I spent my nights at rest stops. When I was getting closer to Dallas, I started watching the air for my "air map" to Love Field. The airplanes guided me right to Love Field. The workers there were all Southern folks. It took a while, but I began fitting in real well. They called me the Yankee for a while, but after working with them for some time, I just fit right in. At that time, Love Field terminal was moved from the north to the east side. American added a lot more flights, so I filled one of the slots American needed. A couple of my buddies also transferred to Lose Field east. I worked the ramp handling bags, mail, and freight, which was a piece of cake. I met a friend that took me under his wing. He had a fishing boat and every time he would go fishing, I would go with him. We started a fishing club that lasted for several years. We had fishing tournaments all over north Texas. I came in first one time. At that time in life, the black folks rode the back of the bus and had their own bathroom. Blacks here, whites there. My fishing buddy got sick and never went back to work On my way back home from work on payday, I would pick up his check for him. He didn't live long after that. He was only in his fifties. He was a very good man, way too young to leave us. That put a finish to our fishing for a while.

I had another friend whose wife worked as a beautician that had a friend who wanted to meet me. I met her at the shop where she worked then we would go out for a bite to eat or something. We did that for some time. After a time, she finally told me she had three boys and that I could meet her at her folks' place. They rented a home by the power plant in Coppel, Texas. Her dad helped build the power plant. Her parents had a house full of people. They had three families living together with her parents—she and her three kids, sister and husband that worked as a co-pilot for Central Airlines and their three kids, and her younger sisters. It was a full house! You would think a person stepping into a situation like that he would step right out the back door. But they all treated me so well I stayed around. I asked her to marry me in 1960. Her dad and mother were in the process of retiring and moving to Sacramento, California. My brother-in-law, the pilot for Central Airlines, bought three acres of land in Grapevine, Texas. He asked us if we wanted to buy an acre that was just next to his. We went to look at it and oh my, it was a jungle. Full of weeds and vines. We bought our one acre for fifteen hundred dollars. I bought an ax, chainsaw, and mower and my spare time was used up cleaning out all the brush on that acre. On an occasion I would run across a copperhead. He did not last very long. When I got it all cleaned up, we went to a loan company for a loan to put a home on the land. The only way I could get a loan was if I had a home on that land. So I went to a used lumber place, bought some lumber, and had them deliver the load to the land. I picked through the lumber, built a sixteen-by-sixteen room, went back to the loan company, and got a loan to put a three-bedroom home on that land. I got a part-time job working for the contractor in Euless, Texas, that was building our house The contractor had an older guy that did all the work for him. He was an older guy that did all the work by himself, and of course, I was part-time help so I helped him. My brother-in-law had a very small home that was on his land when he bought it. So between our sixteen-by-sixteen room and his small house, we somehow made it. The carpenter did not finish the inside of our house, so I did the best I could to finish the inside. The contractor I worked for had a well digger and a back hoe. He dug the well and put in our septic system. I didn't have money to pay for that, so after working for American, I would head to a job the contractor had for me to do to pay off the septic system. One job was very large—tearing down a big church. That was a big job, but I got her done. Each day after working till nearly dark, I would head back to Grapevine Lake where I would jump in and take off the first few layers of dirt, then go home and finish off the rest, have a bit to eat, and go to bed so I could get enough rest to go again the next day. I ended up getting my brother, Kenny to come to Texas to work for our contractor. He lasted for a good long while until he missed his girlfriend so much he had to move back to Iowa. After some months I worked enough to pay for our well and septic system.

When my wife's mom and dad and some of the family left for California, they left their old Chrysler with us. I cut it down and made a pickup out of it. Not long after they got to Sacramento, California, our phone rang. My wife answered, said a couple of words, fell to the floor, and passed out. I took the phone and found out her dad had been run over and killed. He was a real nice guy, but in the last few years he developed something that made his reactions slow. From what they said, he was crossing the street right in front of their house when he got ran over.

After the passing of my father-in-law, my mother-in-law gave piano lessons to support herself and the rest of the family. She did good enough to support my wife's youngest sister that had a half a dozen kids with a half a dozen dads. The sister-in-law did not receive any support from the fathers.

The street we lived on had two homes besides ours. The first one was an older couple. Both drank very heavily and were overweight. He had gout and smoked very heavily and bought the cheapest beer they could find. Their lifestyle fit with my wife's, so she spent a lot of time helping them get rid of their beer and cigs.

At that time in my life I worked evenings. When I returned home after work one night, I went in the house and didn't find my wife. I went outside to find her and heard someone crying. Found her hiding in the yard. I was never sure what she did when I was gone to work. At that time she was pregnant with our firstborn. I tried to talk to her, but she was drunk out of her mind. It took some time, but after a while she said, sobbing "I am afraid that my child is going to die."

I asked, "Why do you say that?" After talking for some time, she finally told me she had a child from her first husband born strangled with a cord wrapped around its neck. I told her it would be all right, carried her into the house, and put her to bed. Then in January I got a call from work that my wife was going to have our baby. I went home at top speed with my '54 Ford, picked her up, and just after leaving our house, her water broke. We had twenty miles to the hospital, so I put the pedal to the metal. There was a "roundabout" just as I was getting into Dallas. It just so happened there was a cop there. I pulled up to him and told him what was happing. He turned on his siren and said, "Follow me." Going as fast as we could, we got to the turn to the hospital and the cop turned left. My wife said to turn right We went right, went a half block, turned around, and followed the cop again. We pulled in to a bunch of nurses greeting us to take her to a room. They got her to a room and left. I went down to find the cop to tell him thanks, but he was long gone. Went back up to the room to where my wife was to find her in a contraction. She had her legs up and a little head sticking out. I called out, "Help! Help! We are having that baby." The help came and so did our baby girt A couple years later a little brother came along. He was born in Grapevine, Texas. That twenty-mile drive a couple years early was just a little much. When he was ready to be born, we had around six inches of straight down snow. To be sure I could get to the hospital, I made tracks down our road because it was not a main road. Sure enough, she was ready to go. I got her to the hospital and held her hand until she was ready to deliver. They sent me out to the waiting room. Everyone in that hospital knew there was a baby being born. I think everyone in Grapevine knew there was a new baby in town. I don't know if ail women scream like that I was really concerned. I did not know what was really happing. After a few hours, our second child was born.

Dad and Mom came from Iowa to visit us that winter. A very embarrassing thing happened when my wife was in the hospital. Wife was getting fitted for a diaphragm while Mom was in her room. There is just no privacy! Mom and Dad stayed for a week and helped with the two children.

For the next ten years, life was really a pistol. There was a dude ranch just up the road from us. I got to know the foreman real well. He and his wife would come over and have a few drinks with us. I bought a boat to go fishing in Grapevine Lake. The sand bass were running at that time of buying my boat. When they would run, it would be early and late days, sometimes in the middle of the day. We would put my boat in the water and wait for the birds to show up (seagulls) where the fish were. Charging out to where the birds were circling, we would start casting our lures in the middle of what looked like the water was boiling. The sand bass would surround the small fish and have their lunch.

One very windy day we went out, just to get away, put the boat in, and started casting one lure, one fish on every cast. We thought one fish on every cast, we could add a torpedo, which was dear. Hook in hack and two on the bottom. In front of that about one foot, we added a yellow jig; in front of that a white jig. With that rig we caught three with every cast. We would go in the cove and let the wind blow us out to the middle of the lake. After a half a dozen trips like that, we ended up with close to a thousand sand has. We did not have a limit at that time in catching sand bass.

The bottom of the boat was covered with fish. We loaded up the boat from the water and stopped the boat under my yard light. My partner had a party at the dude ranch. He had to work, so I ended up cleaning all those fish myself. Got real good at filleting fish—four a minute. That weekend there was not a party at the dude ranch so we had a fish fry there. I started the fish fry. The fish I fried was gone just like that, and the word got around that there was a free fish fry at the dude ranch. I fried fish for at least six hours, ran out of fish, and someone brought me a possum to cook That was my last cooking for that night.

I spent many hours chasing sand bass at Grapevine Lake and Lake Lewisville. I never caught that many fish at one time again. I think that day we depleted the population of sand bass, so the DNR put a limit on sand bass. I set my sights on Lake Lewisville, where I could catch the larger sand bass. I would go after the sand bass catching a dozen or so, go to the shore, fillet my catch, put them on ice, and go for more until I would catch six or seven pounds. I learned how to deep fry, which was the best way for me. Beer batter plus other ingredients.

After our two children got a little older, we spent a lot of weekends at Hippy Comer, which was located on the south end of Lake Arlington. My friend from work at that time of my life was the one that got us to go to Hippy Corner. At Hippy Corner with us was always my friend, his dad, and a bunch of his dad s friends. We had our private party with a fishing boat and barbecue pit. The only black guy they would allow in our group was "Harry Bella La Fante" on the radio. He was our entertainment. After we would change the station and listen to something else. Sometimes I would leave from work and go straight to Hippy Corner. My work friend would pick up my wife and the kids so when I would get there, they would already be there. I never knew what to expect when I arrived. With all that booze that was always there, someone was out of it. At times it was my wife One time she was setting up to the bonfire, fell asleep, and the soles of her boots started to melt. She never said a thing about basing sore feet. I was not real crazy about drinking. I guess I thought I had to drink to keep up with the rest of the world and be a part of her life. So much for that venture in life. I did find time to play some golf and soft ball during that time.

It seems I couldn't please my wife any time. Things always came up short, never had enough money, or something was wrong. With my last dollar, my wife always wanted me to stop at the beer store to pick up a case of beer for our weekend, which was just anytime. That was my mistake and as I look back at things, I should have put a stop to it When I worked from two o'clock to ten in the evening, getting home at ten thirty, all would be quiet. The kids were in bed, and my wife would be in the bathroom with her head hanging over the stool or her head on her arms, set at the table. At first, I would carry her to bed, but after so many times I just left her. One evening when I came home, we had the whole Grapevine police force in my front yard. What happened? My wife's sister's husband had gotten drunk and picked a fight with his wife. He drank a bottle of cream de mint, went out of his mind, got his gun, and was going to shoot anything that moved. His wife had run over to our house with her kids, got in the house, locked the doors, and called 911. They turned out all the lights and hid in the bathroom. With gun in hand, my sister-in-law's husband went around the house, hollering all sorts of things, even cut the telephone line. The police showed up with dogs. He took for the woods and did not get very far before the dogs cornered him. That was not a good evening. We had so many more happenings. Life at that time was not good at all for my family or any family.

In between all the mess of my personal family I was able to do a lot for Mom and Dad because of my airline privileges, which I enjoyed doing, and it gave me a break from all the happenings. I was able to get unlimited tickets for them. They flew out to visit sister Joan, who was in Georgia for a few days. Then to sister Sue's, who was in Virginia. They always enjoyed those trips. Being able to do this for them made me feel so good.

Ten years after our second child was born, we were expecting another baby. Guess what—my wife wanted to abort this child. It took a while for me to get her to understand that was not right to kill an unborn. In time she changed her mind. Our third child was born again in the month of January. He became my shadow as he grew up. He and I did a lot together, golf, put new' shingles on our house, and fished. If I put something down and needed it, he knew just where it was. He came to the top of the house to help me when his mother wasn't home When she was home, we caught some slack because she had some crazy thought that Jr. would fall off the roof One time I was trying to show him how to hold his custom-made golf club and she said, "Leave him alone, so he could do what he wanted." We had to give that up because he wanted to please both of us. My wife was so protective and fearful. Jr really didn't know what he wanted. He was a very good boy.

Lone Rock, my hometown, had their 100th year celebration. I tried to get my family to go with me to celebrate, but my wife just had to go to California and take the whole family with her. She went to California often and took the kids that could go with her The ones in school stayed home with me. I would take a vacation to care for the kids so she could go. She would just say "I'm going," and I had to make arrangements to cover our home front. My life was like that often. I went to Lone Rock's celebration alone. At that time I was forty. Lone Rock decided to get all our family boys to play ball (slow pitch) against the other town boys. When the games were over, we family boys' score was over a hundred, visitors under forty. Dad had a front-row seat to view all the games. He had a few tears watching his boys play their best. That was a highlight of our lives.

Back to Texas, back to work, which was my home away from home. If I could not have gotten along with the people I worked with, I would have been put in the nuthouse.

My buddy from work went overboard (couldn't stop drinking), went to AAA in Hunt, Texas. He came back a different person. We had long talks, so I decided to go also. American Airlines paid the bill. I went to a lot of classes where a lot of people were talking about their life. A lot were drunks, and a lot just had problems that they did not know what to do about in their life, and some just did not give a damn. When I checked in, they put me in a place where if I lost it, they would give me a shot to calm me down. That never happened, so the next day I was able to go where I wanted. There was a volleyball game going on so I just joined in. All that saw me there thought I was one of the staff workers, not a patient. The place was really good for nearly everyone. In classes someone would get up and share his story. I only shared with a couple others. As we would cover the grounds, we talked about what we were going through. Finally this guy said, "Why do you call yourself stupid, dummy, plus other things so much." I did not realize I was doing that. I thought about that and caught myself say it lots of times after he drew to my attention. I still try to think before I say anything. "If you can't say something nice, don't say anything at all."

There were two psychiatrists, one woman, one man. I wanted to be assigned to the woman because she made a lot of sense to me. I got assigned to the man, one hour each day. To me all we did was visit about building and digging wells. Don't see where that did me any good. One day we took off for President Johnson's golf course in Johnson City Texas. That was a good day. They had golf clubs for us with all the works. I talked to some of the golfers on the course. I asked them about Johnson. They said he was a person that cheated worse than anyone that they ever played with. It was a good relaxing day. Back at Hunt, when I had a visit with my psychiatrist, he told me, "When you start standing up for yourself you will find you may lose a lot of your friends and family." The next weekend, my wife flew down and we visited with the lady psychiatrist together. My wife let all her feelings out. She started out on me like the world was coming to an end. She could not say enough terrible things about me. I never had enough money for her and could not do enough for her. I did not say a thing. I just let her talk. I have not a clue why she flew off the handle like that. It did not accomplish a thing. She went home, and I stayed there. I had my fiftieth birthday there. It was a good birthday party with all the so-called misfits. A lot of them went through what I went through. We kind of understood each other. My fiftieth birthday was not that bad. Too bad it took me fifty years to get started to get a direction in my life. When I got home, my wife and I thought maybe if we left Texas things would get better. American Airlines was opening a station in Salt Lake City at that time. I put in for a transfer, got it, and we left for our big change. The three stepsons were all out of school, so they stayed behind and lived in the house. Our three children moved with us. Our oldest son went out for baseball tryouts and made the team. The next day they found out he was not a Mormon so he had to go through another tryout. Needless to say he did not make the team that time.

Out of the blue my dad and mom decided to come out to visit us. They drove all the way to Salt Lake for a visit. I gave them a tour of the area. Bingham Canyon Copper Mine was right there in Utah. The mines were being worked on. I took them up to the top of the mine, which was an open mine. Dad and I walked up to the sightseeing area that overlooked the huge hole in the ground. Dad's health was not good at that time, and he had a real hard time breathing, so we went back to the house. They stayed for a week. Dad was not in good shape, so Mother did all the driving. I do not know if they had a good time or not; they never let me know. I enjoyed basing them there, but it showed me Dad was not in good health at all.

We were not in Salt Lake City very long before I realized the grass was not any greener there than Texas. I knew that was not the answer for us and the kids. I put my transfer in to go back to Texas station, which did not take too long with my seniority. We were in Salt Lake City for nine months. My wife and kids stayed in Salt Lake for school to finish before they came back to join me. When I got back to our house in Grapevine, Texas, it was a junk pile. The stepsons did not care for any part of the house. They had not paid the utility bills. All utilities were turned off; dark curtains all over the place. They had turned it into a place where dope peddlers came to smoke their pot and other stuff.

I just lived in my truck for a time until they got their stuff out of my house. After a few weeks, they got out and moved to another place. When school was out, my wife and kids flew back to Texas. Things did not get any better between wife and myself She got involved in a "cult" group because one of her friends was in. I did go with her a couple of times to see if it would help us. They were trying to get me to believe in reincarnation. I had a hard time with that, so I went looking for self-help books and asking questions to anyone that could give me direction. I could not figure out why my life was so messed up. A couple of guys at work told me if you would start reading the Bible, I would find out how to live and find what my problems were. They told me to go to an open-Bible church. I started going on Sunday mornings and Wednesday nights. After a few times, I found out my frame of mind was sort of out in left field. I got into my Bible every chance I got. I carried the Bible everywhere I went. If I had a question, I had a good friend at work that was a preacher that helped me understand. On his days off he went around to different churches and gave sermons. He gave me information that I could understand. I was beginning to find out why things were all screwed up. I discussed reincarnation with him, and he said, "Once anyone gets into that frame of mind, there is no changing their mind." I knew I was not going there in my life. It did not make since in any way to me!

After a few months of my studying the Bible and going to church, I knew my wife and I needed counseling. I finally talked her into going to a counselor. We went once and all she wanted to do was argue about how wrong my thinking from the Bible was. Soon after that, I found out she had already filed for divorce without saying a thing to me.

At that rime I still had a small Toyota pickup with a topper on it. I had a buddy that had an extra bedroom in a little place north of the airport that I moved to. I did not have to move much because I did not have anything but my personal items. I left all the house belongings for the kids and her.

My Dad passed on December 24, 1979. Went home to the funeral Spent time with family and then back to Texas to try to get order in my life.

After Dad passed, Mom had a friend who lived down the street from her whose husband had passed the day before Dad. Mom and this friend started doing everything together. They enjoyed each other's companionship very much. Her friend had been going to South Texas for a few years with her husband and wanted to continue to do that. The next fall her friend asked Mom if she would like to go with her to Texas for the winter months. It didn't take too much to convince Mom to go to South Texas. They drove her friend's car to South Texas. Mom's friend had rented a small place at Pharr South trailer park in Pharr, Texas.

Before their first month was up, Mom's friend didn't like renting and bought a lot and new mobile home. I made it a point to fly down every so often to visit and help them with whatever their needs were. A couple times I did drive; at that time there was hardly any traffic on the two-lane road once I got off Interstate 35. Before our divorce, the kids' mom did go down to visit one time. She was still trying to decide if she want to be married to me or not. Our divorce was on hold. In fact I was trying to save the marriage even though we were still living separately. Other times I just would come down and play golf and take Mom and her friend to Peter Piper, Stares, DQ, or McDonald's. With all my troubles, I would call Mother. She would say, "Why don't you talk to my friend's daughter that had gone through a divorce?" I knew I wanted to get my life straightened our so I called her a couple times. She told me what books to read—Dobson, etc.—as well as prayer. And not give up until I knew I had done everything possible to save my marriage. I continued to try to get my life in order for about five years. I worked, spent whatever time I could with the kids, went to church, and studied the Bible.

At times in my thoughts I thought maybe if I would get real sick, wife would change her mind. You know the saying, "You don't know what you have until you lose it." Not long after that while at work, not feeling very well, I sat down in the lunch room and leaned against the wall. I heard someone say, "Hutch does not look very well." One of the supervisors said, "I think we better take you to the hospital." My supervisor drove me; my side hurt so bad that every bump in the road was a killer. At the hospital they met me with a wheelchair, then laid me up on a stretcher. I think all the staff had to ask me questions and poked at me. Each time they poked me, talk about hurt. Finally the Doc came in, put his finger on my side, and said, "Is that where it hurts." He hit the spot and said give him a shot of something. Whatever it was it took all the pain away. They had to call wife to come in and sign some papers so they could be operated on for an appendicitis attach. After the shot I felt as if 1 was as good as new. I was wheeled down the hall to the operating room. The operating crew stood around and said good night and stuck a needle in my arm. The next thing I remember was me waking up in a room by myself I felt a lot of pain. A nurse came in to check on me and gave me a pill for pain. The next morning they got me up to walk the hall pushing a stand with a bottle hanging on it with a tube running to my arm. The nurse kind of helped me struggle down the hall. "Hurt, oh, my." My three kids came to visit, but wife never did come until she had to come and check me out of the hospital. Wife did take me back to our house for a short while. I knew from the lack of her concern for me that it was over, and I needed to more on with my life.

American Airlines said that I had to take a month off to recuperate. I called Mom and asked if I could come and visit with her while I rebuilt my strength. I hopped on a plane and went home to recover at Moms. I just hung around doing not a whole lot. At that time, sister Joan was flying to Des Moines, Iowa for a visit also with Mom. I asked Mom's friend to ride into Des Moines with me to pick my sister up. Des Moines is a 3-hour drive from Mom's. Mom's friend's daughter, whom I had visited with by phone a couple times, lived there and she would be able to visit her. My sister was coming in on an eady flight so we decided to go in the night before and stay. Her name is Janece. She met us with a big smile we went out to eat and enjoyed our visit that evening. We had a lot of things in common; our families shared rides back and forth to school, Dads passing a day apart, mothers going to South Texas sharing a home together there and living a block apart in the summertime. We talked until the wee hours of the morning. That was a start of a good understanding of what life was all about. Both of us tried to fix what we thought was wrong with our marriages, to no avail.

Mom's friend's name was Lola, Janece's mother, and I had to lease right away after breakfast to pick up Joan and travel back home. As we were leaving, I asked Janece if it would be all right if I would come in and spent more time with her on my weekends off after I went back to work. She said, "Sure." I found out later from her, she didn't think anything about it because she knew I lived in Dallas, Texas, and she was in Des Moines, Iowa—that was really too far away for it to happen. She had *no* desire to have a relationship with me or any man at that time in her life or ever!

After my month off, I went back to Texas and moved back into my friend's room and started my new direction of life. I had the early-morning shift and weekends off so I called Janece and asked if I could come in that weekend. She gave me her travel schedule and said she would be home and that would be fine for me to come in that Friday late afternoon. I then checked the flights to list myself and found the flights were full, so 1 wouldn't get on Friday. I decided then to take that Friday off because the flights were open for me. I called Janece to tell her I would be in on Thursday eady afternoon instead of Friday and she was not home. I talked to her daughter and told her. Again later Janece told me when she got the message she was upset. She just didn't know who I thought I was to come in a day early without discussing it with her. When she met me at the airport, she didn't seem upset. We had a lovely weekend sharing our life stories. Every chance I got I would fly in on my days off. She was always at the airport with her Silver Bullet, which was an '85 Mark IV. We just had a good time getting to know each other and understanding each other. Janece suggested for me to give Irene another chance to saving our marriage. I went back to Texas and tried to no avail. I had invited her out for dinner and went to pick her up at the beauty salon where she was working. When I got there, she and the other hairdressers were sitting there smoking and having a beer. I commented my disapproval of it and she got upset because she felt I was judging. I knew then this was not going to work. She wanted a different lifestyle then I did. I then went to her lawyer and agreed to all she wanted. She got the car, to live in the house, all new appliances, and kids. I had monthly and every other holiday visiting privileges with our youngest son. I did ask the lawyer about if she inherited from her family, would it be hers and what I inherited from my family was mine. That lawyer said, "Yes, that is the way it is." I did not have the lawyer put that in the divorce papers. I found out that was a mistake later in my life, which I will share later. We signed the divorce papers—final.

Later when it came to my visiting rights with our youngest son, I only got that privilege once. We went out to dinner with his older brother and sister. At that time I asked my oldest son if he wanted to go fishing and hunting in Iowa and Canada. My youngest son asked if he could go also. I told him he sure could. When I called later to set the trip up, my youngest son would not come to the phone to talk to me. I don't know what happened between the dinner and the phone call. I tried to get my visitation honored, but he did not want anything to do with it. I even went to court to get my rights honored. The courts had a psychiatrist test myself and ex-wife. The result came back as I was okay and ex-wife was like a snake full of venom, ready to bit at any time. It ended up with the judge telling her she had to honor the visitation or go to jail She chose to not honor the visitation, and I decided putting the kids' Mom in jail was not wise. So I stepped aside and prayed that someday they'd choose to be a part of my life. I don't know what happened to him because we got along very fine and did a lot together before. I do know the kids' mother had a lot of control over them and their choices. Their mother was very protective of them. My first born son is a lot like me, quiet and a hard worker. He has always turned to me for direction in his life. We would discuss his direction for his career, how he could get a pickup financed, etc. He was always a hard worker and worked very hard at whatever he was doing. I have to say he is a lot like me, and I am proud of him. I would like to say the other two are the same, but I have not gotten to be an active part of their lives because of their mother. They have chosen to not be a part of my life. My daughter has come around a little, but still not at ease. I leave this in our Lord's hands.

I continued to go into Des Moines, visiting Janece for the next year. Janece had a decorating business and traveled a lot, so I had to work out the time when she was in the city During these visits, I knew I wanted to be a more active part of her life. I told her I could transfer to Des Moines. She told me that would be fine if I wanted to so I could be closer to my family and not on her account. She told me she had not any plans to remarry. So I didn't put in for the transfer. I kept going in for visits through November, the time of her birthday. Janece's youngest daughter at home was a junior in high school. She told Janece before she left for school this particular Friday that she would not come home that night because she was going to spend the night with her gidfriend. Janece questioned that and asked her what she was planning to do that she did not want her mother to know about Her daughter got upset and it was just left at that. She was going to stay with a friend that night. Janece picked me up at the airport and we went out to dinner that evening and were back at the house watching TV. Janece received a call from the local police department asking whether she had a daughter and naming her daughter. Janece was surprised about the call and asked the police to repeat that statement. The policeman did and got a little upset and asked if this was Janece XXX. The policeman said Janece was to come and get her daughter Getting there, Janece found out her daughter was with other girlfriends and were driving to a party and got stopped for not stopping at a stop sign. They happen to have an open can of beer in the back seat. When Janece got back, she asked me to leave and go back to Dallas. She needed to spend time with her daughter. I got myself on the early-morning flight for the next morning and left. I did have to borrow a suitcase from Janece because I had left clothing there each time I would visit instead of carrying them back and forth. Janece told me to take everything home with me. I thought she was telling me she did not want to see me anymore. I was disappointed but did what she asked. She had told me early on that the most important part of her life at that time was her daughter and her graduation and college.

I continued working my job at Dallas. I knew Janece was coming to Dallas on business the middle of December. I called her and told her I would meet her at the airport and give her the suitcase back I had used to get my clothes back the month before. She said, "Fine." I met her and four other ladies at the luggage department. I watched them get their luggage and thought, What did they rent to drive to transport all this luggage? They each had two large suitcases. I offered to help them get it to the hotel. Janece told me no, that would be fine, because she had rented a big town car to handle it all. After she said that, I asked her if she was sure she could get everyone in as well as the luggage. At that time she looked at all the luggage and reality sat in. I helped them get everything to the hotel! As I was leaving them, the other ladies said they would like to take me to the restaurant for ice cream. I accepted. I never turned down ice cream. I enjoyed getting to know more of Janece's business friends and left for the evening. The next day Janece and her business friends shopped at their warehouse for whatever merchandise they wanted at a very special price. By the time they had finished and gathered ar the departure door, they found they had way too many boxes to travel in their car again. Her friends suggested calling me again for help. Janece did, but I was not home from work yet. She left a message and I called her when I got home. They' really were not far from me. I loaded ten large boxes in my pickup and was going to take it to my friend's garage and found out it was way too much for his garage. I then thought I would just take it to the airport and send it out on the next plane to Des Moines. That did not work either because they were not going to be on that flight. So I ended up taking it to their hotel rooms for them. As I was leaving, Janece's friends told me I could come the next day and spend the day with Janece. So I told Janece I would see her the next day. She was a little upset with her friends. She said no, that was their shopping day at the malls. Her friends continued to say they didn't want her with them. She gave in and said fine, but I would be going to all the malls and shopping places she wanted to go. She showed me places I didn't even know we had in the Dallas area. And she knew her way around like she lived there, better than myself living in the area Midafternoon I told Janece I wanted to take her to a nice place for dinner that evening and asked her if she knew of at place. She said, "Yes, the Reunion Tower would be nice." I knew where it was so we went there for dinner that evening. To my surprise as we were getting off the elevator to enter the restaurant, a lady started talking with Janece. Here she is miles away from where she lives and knows someone in Dallas, Texas, and I live here and didn't know anyone all day and evening. We had a nice dinner and enjoyed each other's company. At that time I told her, "This would be a nice place to…," and she interrupted me and told me not to spoil a wonderful day. We went back to the hotel and visited a little. When I left, I took all their boxes with me. We had agreed to meet at a certain time at the airport to get their boxes with them and their luggage. They were going to church with the owner of the company Janece contracted to.

That next morning I received a call from Janece telling me they had been invited to brunch at the Fairmont Hotel from Janece's boss and so it would be very close to our meeting time for the luggage. (I found it interesting, motivational speaker, Zig Zigglar, was the person that Janece talked with to find the phone to call me that morning.) I waited for them at the agreed place and time and they didn't come, so I went ahead and took the boxes and checked them in on their flight. I was able to do that because their names were on the list that day for flight. I then went to the gate and waited for them. They were running late and Janece dropped off her friends. She still had to take the rented car back She told them to go ahead and check in and if she wasn't there, she would have to catch the next flight. I greeted each of them and found out what was happening. Just as the plane door was to be shut, Janece came running up, said thanks, and got on the plane.

Janece and I didn't talk again until the holidays after that. I called her to wish her a happy holiday and we visited. She sounded blue and lonely. I tried to talk her into flying to South Texas to visit our moms in January. She said she couldn't afford it. I told her I would send her a ticket. Of course, she wouldn't accept it. Her mother called and offered to pay for her ticket. She finally gave in and I sent her a ticket. I also sent a ticket to my brother, Pete, and his wife to come down at the same time. We all met in Dallas and flew to McAllen together. We had a great time. Janece told me later that she knew I would ask her to marry again this trip, and she was going to accept. I had done that a few times already, and she had told me to not ask her again. She just wanted to be friends. So I let up on it. This trip I did feel she was a little different toward me.

When we left to go home that weekend, Janece got on the flight and I didn't. She had a ticket and I was flying standby. We were planning on having dinner at the Dallas airport, and of course with me not getting on the plane stopped that from happening. I noticed Janece was a little upset that I didn't get on. But I didn't know why.

I called and asked to come in to visit Janece again in February. We went out to dinner and watched a movie on TV at the house. I was on the floor getting a fire built in the fireplace and just said, "I don't know why you wouldn't marry me."

She said, "I will."

I turned around and said, "I don't think you understood what I said." She said she knew what I said and yes, she would marry me.

Janece did not want to move to Dallas, so I put in for a transfer to Des Moines. She also did not want to plan any part of our wedding until after June 1 because of her daughter's graduation. My transfer did not take long for that to happen. I loaded up my Toyota pickup and went back north to Des Moines. At that time another guy transferred also. We got together and shared an apartment at the Warren House in West Des Moines, Iowa.

Janece, having been married the first time in the Catholic church, had gone in to begin her annulment that January. She had to answer a lot of questions about her first marriage. When she finished, the priest told her the way she answered the question she most likely would not get an annulment. Janece just told him that would be the Catholic Church's loss and her God knew she tried to keep her first marriage together and she would find another church that she would be comfortable in. The priest agreed with her on that. He also told her it could take up to three years to hear anything. Janece said fine and left knowing she wasn't planning on doing anything until her daughter graduated that June anyway.

I continued my position with American Airlines in Des Moines and spent as much time with Janece, our families, and her business activities. She wanted me to understand the busyness of her business before we married.

Sunday, June 1, came and her daughter had a wonderful graduation celebration. Then that following Monday, Janece received a call from her priest telling her he had her annulment papers in his hands, signed and sealed. He also said he had not experienced this fast of an annulment in his career. That then began our plans for our wedding day and life together as husband and wife. I, being Catholic but not marrying in the church the first time, did not have to go through an annulment. My paperwork was very easy.

We went to her church in West Des Moines and began our time with the priest there. The first time we visited with him before the annulment went through, he was very cool with us and told us he didn't need to talk with us until the annulment was complete. When we called him, he was also very surprised with the short time it took. We planned a September 13 wedding day and spent several times with the priest, which were very enjoyable. In fact the priest asked us to help work with the engaged couples at the church after we were married, and we did for several years. We enjoyed it very much.

Of course, our mothers were very excited for us. We planned a lovely mass wedding with all our family and friends. Bill was our best man, and Duane was our second groomsman. Janece's son walked her down the aisle and her two daughters were the bridesmaids. We had beautiful music.

We than invited all of them to our home for a reception. Janece's sister, brother, and their mates, along with our mothers, took care of all the serving. We had all the food delivered to the house.

We had a house full of well-wishers. My whole family came, except Sue and Joan. All of Janece's family was there. There were a lot of old schoolmates that even showed up. Everyone showed up from our home-town Lone Rocker, as well as from home interiors, American Airlines, and many dear, dear friends.

We enjoyed greeting everyone until it was time for us to leave for the airport. Our mothers had a limousine set up to take us out to the airport for our trip to Florida. Our mothers followed us out to the airport to give us their wishes for a good life together.

We flew from Des Moines to Dallas, spent the night at the Airport Hotel, and then the next morning on to Fort Lauderdale, Florida. We rented a car to drive to Fort Myers, Florida. Our trip was on Alligator Alley, driving across Florida to our hotel in Naples, Florida, right on the oceanside. On the other side of our hotel was a golf course. Breaklast at the hotel, golf across the street, Village Inn for lunch. Down the street was Tin City. This is a very popular place for shopping; Of course we had to shop. Golf in the morning and beach in the afternoon then on to shop in the evening.

A week later, back to reality: Janece went back to her home interiors business and I went back to work at American Airlines in Des Moines.

We would go up to visit our moms a couple times a month and take them to meals as well as take them to Kansas, Minnesota, Virginia, and Georgia to see a few of my brothers and sisters.

Every year we went to South Texas to visit our mothers and get away from the cold winter. We would take our golf clubs and play as much golf as we could. When golf finished for the day, we would take our mothers out to their favorite place for lunch. Stars, DQ, Peter Piper, or maybe even McDonnell's. We really didn't see much of them because they had to shuffle, play cards, or even bingo at several parks. Maybe you might find them at the pool hall.

We thought maybe we would give the family a trip to go to South Texas. We started with Bill and his wife Of course they didn't turn that down. I guess they had a good time because they came back for several years. For a few years after that, Bill and wife stayed with mother and Lola and said that was the cheapest vacations he has ever had. Pete was next, but that year he had a heart attract. We suggested to Mom if she wanted to go see Pete, we would take her to Great Bend, Kansas. Well, Bill brought her to Des Moines. With that we had to invite Bill and his wife to ride along. When we got to Great Bend, we stayed a couple days, and went back Later that year when Pete got better, I got tickets for him and his wife to fly to South Texas to visit Mom. Pete did give me a hundred dollars to cover my expenses. We also arranged for all the family to come to South Texas to see their mother. Only three took advantage of that gift from me. I am not sure what year Sue's husband passed, and American Airlines came through again. I got tickets for Mom, Bill, and his wife. The rest of the family could not make the funeral, except for Bud—I guess he just didn't want to be owing me anything. I rented a car in Dulles and drove to their home in Virginia. Sue asked Janece if she would say the eulogy. She said okay and I just needed to give her all the information that she needed to put together for the eulogy. All went well. We did the funeral and went back to West Des Moines.

We joined Echo Valley golf club because we got a good deal because they needed a few more golfers. Janece took some lessons and got to enjoy golf very much. At that time I worked six to two thirty. Echo Valley was just south of the airport, so I would go from work to the golf course. I met a couple good old boys on the golf course, Larry and Ed. We played a lot of golf together I retired in 1995 and was looking for something more to do, so we bought ten acres ten miles south of Winterset, Iowa— Podunk, Iowa, which is located ten miles south of Winterset, Iowa. One day Ed said, "How about playing softball?"

"Sure, I would like to give it a try." I am still playing, which started 2002. Ed got hit on the shin bone and had to give softball up for golf.

I had to give up Echo Valley because I was involved in redoing the ten acres. Bought an old Caterpillar with a large bucket to move dirt to make a fishing pond. On our way back from Lone Rock, we spotted a small house-trailer in a small town, stopped and asked how much they needed for that trailer. They only wanted a couple hundred, so we bought it. Instead of running back and forth from home to our small firm, I had a place to sleep. For two summers I moved dirt, making a pond the size of a football field. Finished the large, and just for something more to do, I built three small ponds. With all the black dirt from the draw, I set that aside to make a garden with all that good dirt. I cut through a small hill for my overflow. My tool for leveling was an eight-inch level. Work a couple of weeks got my level out to check my next step. I only got my cat stuck three times. Had a good neighbor that pulled me out. The first time he charged me a hundred bucks, after that he just came and pulled me out. He just liked to come and see me to see what I was up to next. The next spring I and myself built a barn, sixteen-by-twenty, with a loft. I had a friend that had a mill that milled me a truckload of one-by-fours rough cut oak I used for my paneling. I paneled floor to ceiling, including the celling. Upstairs, for the floor, I used plywood and covered that with carper With all the insulation and carpet, that place stayed cool in the summer and warm in the winter. With the pond done, along came fall then winter We would take the grandkids out to play in the snow and slide down the hill where I piled up extra dirt from the pond.

On that over flow I built a covered bridge (to tie in with the covered bridges of Madison County where our ten acres were) that went from one part of my garden to the other. The bridge is twenty feet long and six wide, seven feet tall with covered roof and sides. The second spring I went out to move more dirt. Just getting started, I uncovered a large bubble bee home. When I started to move some dirt, that really started to upset those bees. I turned off the Caterpillar and set still for a couple hours until the bees settled down. I carefully crept the opposite direction, got in my truck, and went home. Told Janece what was happening. In the morning I was taking my shotgun out to clean out the bees. I used up quite a few shells but cleaned out the bees, leveled the garden, and sold my cat to my friend that milled the wood for me.

When spring came, the pond filled up as I planned. Put in a garden around one-half acre that produced all we could eat plus giveaway. With a little dirt hoe and some seed and a little sweat, a little garden goes a long way. I stocked my pond with a lot of the neighbor's pond that had black bass, crappie, and blue gill. Went to a small creek and seined a bunch of minnows for a feast for my fish. After all of that land scraping, we decided to build a six-bedroom home. We found a contractor in Creston, Iowa, that drew up a contract for our six-bedroom home. Of course the contractor and his wife had to come out to get a picture of what he had to work with. On our walk around the land, we walked by a pile of dirt. Standing by the dirt, the contractor's wife saw a huge bull snake, turned, and ran over Janece, knocking her flat to the ground. When Janece struggled to her feet, she had grass in her glasses and her black-and-white pant suit was full of grass stain. The contractor said, "You should be moved in before the snow flies." Janece and I spent our Christmas and New Year's painting the inside.

Snow came and our house was not finished. After a few calls, we talked to him about things that were not up to standard. The contractor was kind of giving us some slack. Janece was a little upset and said if it is not fixed to our satisfaction, you can take it back That really got him upset. He went into Winterset, Iowa, and put a lean on our place. He did come back and fixed it up to our satisfaction.

While I am on this subject, I will finish this venture.

I don't think I said anything about me jumping off the Cat and caught my ring finger, putting a huge gash in it. I ran the Cat for a couple more hours then deckled to go home and have Janece clean it up. When I walked into her office, I said, "Don't faint. Just come home and clean it up for me."

She said, "No way! You are going to a doctor." She dragged me to the doctor He wanted to cut my wedding ring off. "No, work around my ring," I said. He did and finally ended up putting six stitches in my ring finger.

Janece was the designated mower for the acres that could be mowed. Janece had to make our ten acres look good because she had her home interiors retreats and Christmas parties. I did a lot of preparing meals for the girls. On one home interior function, they had been up for lunch and I was cleaning up after all the ladies went on down to their afternoon meeting. I went to bum trash that was located on the north side of our pond. I started my trash burning and watched it until I thought the fire was out. I went to get my truck and started to town to get our supplies for our evening dinner As I was leaving, I looked toward where my bonfire was and saw the fence line burning! I stopped my truck and ran down to the fire It was a little too much for me. I ran to the bam to get a bucket to dip water from my stream that was not too far away. I was trying my best to do what I had to do. In the house, Janece was holding the meeting. In the lower level where the meetings were held, we had all windows looking out onto our large pond, the barn, and northeast toward the burn pile. One of the directors interrupted Janece and asked, "Is Don jogging?" Janece just said *no* and continued the meeting. In a little bit, she asked again if Don jogged Janece again said *no* and continued. The director then said "Are you sure Don doesn't need help?" Janece looked up, a litde upset, and saw the fire and Don running to the barn. She and the seven directors jumped up, grabbed buckets from the garage, and ran to help. Of course they were all dressed in business attire, and one even had a long skirt. We had rakes, shovels, and buckets trying to put the fire out. A few of them created a bucket brigade from the creek to the fire. Janece called 911 and they knew right where we were located. Because of the location of the fire on the property, rhe fire truck had to come through the neighbor's field, so one of the ladies climbed over the fence and ran up to the gate to let them in. Another one of the ladies drew her long skirt up between her legs and tucked it into her waist, and then climbed over the fence to put the fire out on that other side. What was also interesting about the two that went over the fence was the top two lines of wire was barbwire! Didn't bother a bit!

By the time the fire truck got there, we pretty much had the fire under control. The firemen saw me with all the women dressed in business attire that had buckets, rakes, shovels, etc. They smiled and said, "You ladies are a little overdressed to be fighting a fire, aren't you?" This was late summer and it was a very dry summer. If we had not put that fire out, it would have burned acres and acres of properties. What was interesting about the one asking Janece about me jogging was she had seen me running from the truck, which I had parked on the road, when I noticed the fire had started up again because of the wind picking up. Needless to say, that event put a little damper on the meeting for the rest of the day! Another exciting memory in my fife, this time in Podunk, Iowa.

The next year, we had a get-together, family and friends. (We had at least one each year after I got the barn built before the house was built.) Lots of family members showed up for the first one. The second one was after we built our six-bedroom home. Mom and all of the sisters and brothers, except the youngest, were there as well as some of their children. We played cards with Mom as much as we could. She enjoyed these times together. She was in her mid-eighties at the time. We had it all, I thought. I found out later that my oldest brother had his finger in what was not his. I will explain later With all the time we put in that, it was time for someone else to enjoy our ten acres. At that time, I started to get involved in softball. With all time I was putting into that farm, I had no time for not much else. It did not take too long to sell. We sold at the right time because the next year, the bottom fell out of real estate. What we could not sell or give to kids, we gave to the Winterset Catholic Church, which was a lot. The church people came out and loaded up everything we gave them. After all these years, we have not gone back to see what it looks like. I guess that's all right because we do not want to be disappointed.

I am going to try to put together our moms' trips to Texas. Lola and George, Janece's parents, rented in South Texas for a few years until George passed the day before Dad passed. Lola and Mom became great companions after that. Lola invited Mom to go with her, and Mom decided to go south for the winter Lola rented for a while then decided to purchase lot 125 and bought a new trailer for the lot for the two of them to live in. Lola and Mom drove together for nine years until Lola passed. Mom rented from Lola for a hundred bucks a month, which was very inexpensive living monthly. After Lola's passing, Janece asked her sister and brother if they minded offering Emma a contract to continue going down since she enjoyed it so for the nine years with their mom. Janece didn't want Emma to start living in the cold Iowa winter after being out of it or nine years. Bill would come to South Texas for some winter vacations and stay with our moms. When Janece and I would come and visit, Bill would go to Kingsville, Texas, so we could have the second bedroom. Mom and Lola bunked up together at those times. Sometimes, Bill and his wife would stay and sleep on the hide-a-bed. One time when Janece was visiting her mother, she told Janece, "Before Emma passes, she will have a very sad happening with her children." Janece did not question her mother She just knew that her mother was concerned about her friend, Emma. Later, we found out from Janece's sister that Lola had told Jane that Bill will not stay' at her trailer ever again. Of course, Janece did not think much about that statement from her mother until a happening with Bill, which I will go in detail later in the book. And at that time was when her sister shared the statement Lola had told her The same statements were made to the two of them in February of 1989 just before Lola passed in June of 1989. Another statement came from our neighbor, Frank. He said, at times he would witness Bill shaking his finger at Mom when they were sitting in the car and when he would stand on the porch of the mobile home. I asked myself, why would Bill do that to Mom? Many times Bill would say to Mom, "I don't know how I am going to buy the farmland from each of my brothers when you die." Then he would say, "Mom, I am so proud of my brothers and sisters; they are so successful." He also would tell her he just didn't know how he was going to make it He was always having a bad farming year. He keep Mom in the mindset of the hard times that she and Dad went through when they were starting out with all us kids. When Uncle Dean passed, Dad's brother, we found out he gave all the nieces and nephews ten thousand dollars each. Uncle Dean never married, so we were his family. Mom never did like Dean. One time when I was with Mom in South Texas, we were talking and I said to Mom that Dean was not such a bad person after all; just look what he gave to all of us. *Ten thousand dollars.* That statement made her so upset that she went storming back to her bedroom saying, "All you guys are just waiting for me to die." I still do not know why that set her oft so much She stormed to her bedroom and never came out the rest of the evening. I was so concerned for Mom and didn't know what to do, so I went and visited a couple of friends of ours, in the park here in South Texas at that time and told them what had just happened. I called Janece and told her what happened and that I think I needed some help taking Mom back to Iowa. Janece canceled her next couple of days of meetings to fly down and help me with mother. Janece flew down the next day. When Mom saw her, she was surprised that Janece was there. Janece told her that I was concerned about her and wanted me to come down and help him. We went out to supper with Mom, my brother Pete, and his wife. Mom was upset with them because of a happening of words about Bill earlier that day. She didn't talk to them during supper. She mainly talked to Janece. The next day, we got on our flight to Des Moines with a stop at Dallas. On the way to Dallas, we flew first-class. Janece and Mom sat together, and I sat across from them. When we got into the air, Mom asked Janece when she was going to go back to work. Janece told her, when she knew she was okay. All of us kids had just found out that our mother had sold the rest of the farm to our oldest brother, Bill, without talking to them, which was very upsetting to us because Mom was over ninety years old. Mom then told Janece that it was not her or Bill's fault that she had to pay capital gains for selling the land to Bill. Janece explained to her it was not fair to the other kids to sell the land to Bill without talking to them about it because of her being ninety years old, and if Bill would have waited until after she passed, it would have fallen into the "Step Up" program. She became upset and Janece explained to her that the lawyer and accountant would have told her and Bill about the capital gains because they would not have left them open to a lawsuit. Janece had a good understanding of what was bothering her. Mom kept telling Janece that she could sell her land to anyone she wanted and for any amount she wanted. Janece told her she was right. It just *appeared* that she loved Bill more than the others by not discussing it with them. With her age, it was really part of her estate. Mom would always listen to Janece's logic, but she just would always defend Bill. We had a couple hours in Dallas before we got on our flight to Des Moines. When we got to Des Moines, we told her we would be spending the night and Janece had some business to handle before we left for Lone Rock. In a conversation, Mom told Janece that Dad's will had a life estate of 115 acres for her until she passed, and then it passed to the eleven children. Emma thought it was her land to do whatever she wanted, so Don got his copy of the will to show her how it really read. She was okay with that then. One of Janece's business needs before we left was with her financial adviser. When he came, Janece introduced him to Mom. He knew she sharecropped with Bill and started visiting her on farming. In the conversation, he asked her if she had been getting some good government checks from her corn. She told him *no* because she always took the beans and Bill would take the corn. He was surprised and told her he had not ever heard of that style of sharecropping. Mom told him they did it that way because Bill told her it would be easier that way.

After Janece finished her business, we drove her to Lone Rock. Usually when we would bring Mom home from South Texas, Bill would drive in and drive her for the rest of the way to Lone Rock. This time, he could not do that, so we took her Bill had left South Texas a few days earlier with Moms car and her things because he had traveled home with his car earlier for his wife's sisters funeral and flew back. When we got Mom home, we went in the house to find all the things that Bill took from Texas were stacked in the kitchen. He did not even have the smarts to put the things away for Mom. Janece and I started putting the things away and when we got finished, I told Mom that everything was put away and all she had to do was put away her personal suitcase and she could start playing cards and bingo with her friends. Mom said, "No, we have a family problem and we are going to get this straightened out." Mom left the room, brought some paperwork, and gave it to Janece. She said, "This is what I have that explains everything that has happened." Janece started reading. What was a large surprise to us, and even to mother, was that the first letter Janece read was from the lawyer stating that he and the accountant did not suggest Emma to sell the land to Bill because of her age and because she did not discuss it with the other ten children. She should not carry' a twenty-year contract for him and she would have to report the gift of $700 per acre to the federal government as a gift because she was selling the land for that much under market value. As Janece read this, she asked Mom if she read this before she signed the papers. Mom just looked at her, and from the look we knew Atom had not. She had just trusted her son, Bill. Just as that happened, Bill and his wife walked in. Janece looked at them and told Bill that he needed to correct this matter as soon as possible or it will destroy the family. I was sitting across the table from Mom, and she was going through her mail and interacting with me about her mail like nothing else was happening in the room. Bill told Janece that the letter did not mean anything and then got right in his mother's free and yelled, "We have a deal." As soon as Bill did that, Moms disposition changed and she continued to open her mail and talked with me about it. She acted like nothing was happening around us. Janece was trying to talk sense to Bill. He just got angrier and started yelling at Janece. Janece told him that he needed to go to the bank and get the money to pay off the twenty-year contract, call each of his brothers and sisters to make things right with them, and pay the money from the capital gains back to his mother Janece then turned to his wife and told her that she needed to make sure that he never talked to his mother like that again. She looked at Janece with tears in her eyes and said, "We go through this all the time." Janece told her anyone should never have to go through that ever. Janece told Bill that if she *ever* saw him talking to his mom like that again, she would turn him in for verbal abuse so fast he wouldn't know what happened. There was no talking sense with Bill, so Janece and I left (which we regret to this day). We went to my brother Duane's house and told him what we had just experienced and discussed what we needed to do. We decided to have a conference call with all our brothers and sisters so they all heard the same thing at the same time. We did that and they were all very upset and wanted to get things straightened out.

Things kind of got a little quiet for a while. Later, Pete, Kenny, Duane, and I got together in Lone Rock and decided to go out to the farm and have a talk with Bill about the fix he got the family in. Bill said that Lola willed to Mom the opportunity for her to stay in the trailer in South Texas as long as she wanted to go south for the winter. I told Bill that was not true. Bill got really upset, calling me a liar. Duane responded by slamming his fist on the table and said that was not called for. Then Bill said that I have all the farm information in my computer to check out. All that information was set up by our brother, Dale, and he did not have a clue on how to set up a farming system. If he did, I would think that he would send each of the brothers and sisters all the information on the so-called family farm. Bill wanted to have his son come in and explain more of what was going on. We told Bill, "No, this is just between us kids, not grandchildren." As we were leaving the meeting at Bill's house, he held Kenny back and told him that if we kept asking questions, he would be out *big bucks*. We found out later what he meant by that statement. Stay with us, it will come out later. The next morning, I was with Mom back to town and Bill came in. I asked him if I could see that will he was talking about in Lola's will. He went and got the so-called will. I looked at it, and right at the bottom of the page was

Janece's sisters name and signature. Janece, her sister, and brother, Lola's children, wrote up a legal paper that said that Emma could stay in their trailer if she wanted as long as she agreed to pay the taxes, insurance, and park dues. They would repair any large items that needed. A year later, Janece and I bought them out.

We kept the same contract with Mom. Mom did cover some small needs because she wanted to. One time she had the roof of the trailer coated with a weatherproofing material. She paid them by check and shortly after they left, it rained and all the weatherproofing ran off the trailer. She called and stopped payment because it surely did not work Within the month after that, Mom began getting calls from a check cashing office telling her she owed them the dollar amount of the check. She would tell them she did not because the service the party did for her did not work and she stopped payment on the check. What had happened was the party went to this check cashing company right away after receiving it and got his cash. With Mom stopping payment to the check right away left the check cashing office without their money, and they could not go back and get it from the service party. After a few calls from the person trying to get their money, Mom called me and asked for help in getting them to stop calling her. We had our son-in-law lawyer call them and told them to stop calling and harassing an eighty-five-year-old lady; if they did not, legal action will be taken. Mom never heard from them again. The last couple years of Mom living in South Texas, I covered the expenses and released Mom from the contract. The last two years before Mom stopped coming to Texas, we took over the taxes, insurance, and dues. She had no expense because I drove her car from Iowa to Texas. After she could not travel on the road without stopping for a bathroom break or lunch break, Janece would fly her down and I would drive her car. Thanks to American Airlines for giving that privilege to me for the time I put in with them. All the years we did this, we never had a problem with getting her to and from Des Moines and Texas. On one of our travels, she told me, "Because of what you and Janece have done for me, I am giving you more than the rest of the family. When I pass, you will not have to worry about any money."

Not long after Janece and I got married, Mom told me that my ex-wife's name was on some land and wanted to go to the courthouse to get her name off that land. We got in the courthouse and told them what we wanted to do. They went and got the paperwork and said that we could not take her name off that land without her signature. We left the courthouse and later I was discussing that with Bill. I do not know if he had a clue about that, but he said my ex-wife would probably be dead before Mom does, so don't be concerned about that. Later, we found out that this land her name was on had been deeded to all of us and our mates in 1979 and 1980 and was not ever told that we owned it.

Before I forget another situation, a cousin took an uncle and aunt of ours for around a million dollars. After this cousin's lather passed, he thought he owned the family form. I don't think he got all the land. He did get all of our uncle's land. As the story goes, he intimidated my uncle and aunt until they became afraid of him. Sounded like he had them change their wills, so he got it all. He even told his mother that she was going to hell My brother Bill then said it is no use to go help our uncle and aunt anymore because our cousin has that all sewed up.

One year, Dad reached a time in his life, at an eady age, he could not form. So brother Joe took off from his work to help Dad catch up with his forming. After they got all caught up. Bill told Joe to go back to his Job because he was farming this land. Joe was one of the best when it came to forming, and should have had the chance to form that land just as much as Bill. Back in 2001 or about that time, Mom had to have a hip replacement. Janece and I took her to the hospital to have that surgery even though we lived in West Des Moines and Bill lived within a mile from Mom. On the stretcher, she said, "I have put your name on things that the hospital requires of me." She said if I don't come through this operation, don't be like your cousin. (She was referring to my cousin that messed up his family.)

One day, Janece and I went to the courthouse, started going through paperwork, and got copies of things with my' name listed on them. We found out that we owned land since 1979 and 1980 and didn't know it. This was 2006 when we realized it!

That summer, we—Pete, Kenny, Joe, and their wives—went to Branson for a show and a vacation. Ken had been told about a year before this date that he had a rare dementia. He was still able to golf and did well, but was losing his ability to communicate, understand, and challenged in eating his food. He didn't enjoy the shows that much because he could not understand what they were saying.

Kenny's daughter was so heavy with her father's health challenges and the family's challenges that she sent a letter to her cousin to try to get her to understand and for help.

Letter follows.

Ann, (Bud's daughter)

I want to share some information that I have learned regarding the family affairs that I thought you should be aware of My dad and mom, Don and Janece, Duane, Joe, and their wives all feel very strongly that Bill has been verbally abusive to Grandma for several years. These are some of the reasons why:

Janece and Don were visiting Grandma about five to six years ago when Grandma showed Janece a letter she received from Bill's lawyer. The letter stated that Bill's lawyer did not feel that it was in her best interest to sell her land to Bill because of her age, not being legally represented, and because the other brothers and sisters had not been notified. During this time, Bill came in and saw Janece with this letter, and that is when he got in Grandmas face and yelled at her telling her that they had a deal. Janece was very upset that Bill did this to his mother and told him never to do that again. Janece also looked at his wife and told her never to let Bill talk to his mother that way again and that nobody needed to live like that. Bill's wife had tears in her eyes and said that this happens all the time. After this happened, Janece and Don noticed that Grandma totally changed and started interacting with Don at the table like nothing else was happening in the room. At the same time, Janece was trying to get Bill to understand that he needed to correct this and make it right with all of the family members, or this was going to destroy the family. There was no way Janece could reason with Bill or get him to understand that he needed to correct this. After this happened, Don and Janece made a conference call to all the brothers and sisters, except for Bill and Grandma. They explained to them all exactly what had happened and told them it was in their hands as to what they thought they should do. My dad, Don, Joe, and Duane knew it to be true and were upset with Bill. The other seven have chosen to let it go. I'll give you a copy if you would like. It stated in there how Grandma no longer felt comfortable around Janece. With Grandma being so uncomfortable with Janece and irritated so often, Janece then just said to Grandma that it appears you're not happy here with us any longer, so maybe you do need to go and live with Bill. After that conference call, Bill immediately told everyone that Janece kicked Grandma out. That was not the case. There again, he's got everyone now looking at Janece as the bad person so that no one is looking at him as the bad person. Not any of the seven cared enough to call Don and Janece to get their side of the story. My dad, Joe, and Duane called to get Don and Janece's side of the story. Pete and his wife knew what was going on also but chose to not support Don and Janece to confirm the truth. (There are *always* two sides to every story).

I know for a fact that Bill has a very bad reputation in the Lone Rock and Bancroft area. I have relatives in that area and they say he is a dirty dealer and not to be trusted. My cousin, who is a classmate of two of Bill's sons, witnessed something in high school and has told us that Bill is a mean SOB.

I often think of our cousin, Bill's daughter who left home at the age of sixteen and has hardly ever come home to visit. I know there was something there—why doesn't she come back to visit? She married the boy who was related to Janece's ex-husband at the time and she has told them some very disturbing things about Bill If you really want to know facts, I encourage you to call Don and Janece and get their side of the story. What has happened through the years is that Bill has been successful in turning Grandma and some of the other family members against Janece. That is what verbal abusers do. I've been researching this and the abuse will always do whatever they can (even lie) to protect their abuser. I truly believe that he has succeeded in damaging this family. He got the land that he wanted and he now has the seven believing that Janece is the bad one, not him. I've also read how abusers are like con artists. I'm sure he is very good to Grandma now. He puts on a good act when everyone is around to make it look like he takes good care of Grandma. He knows exactly what he is doing.

Duane and his wife lived across the street from Grandma for several years. They, too, could tell you some stories. I encourage you to make a phone call to them also if you have any doubts.

I have a signed letter from Frank XXXX who was Grandmas neighbor in Texas and who watched out for Grandma and did many things for her. When this family mess came about, he was very upset, wrote a letter, and signed it stating that he watched from his window numerous times Bill shaking his finger at Grandma while they were either in his car or on the steps of her trailer He said he would talk to any of the family and tell them what he knows. He does not lie. His phone number is: #######. This letter was signed in 2008, and Don and Janece shared what Frank had told them to Dale. (Dale was handling matters for his mom.) I don't know if anyone else was made aware of it, but obviously it didn't seem to matter to Dale. Dale told Janece that she was making a mountain out of a molehill and he felt she exaggerated and fabricated things.

I also have a signed copy of the deed of land sale to Don's ex-wife with Ed's (Bill's oldest son) signature dated October 22 for those that do not believe that they (Bill and Ed) bought that land to someone who hasn't been in this family for many, many years. Don personally told Dale that he was working with a lawyer to get his ex-wife's name off the land, but instead they bought her out anyway. They could have at least called Don and talked to him of the situation, and that they were going to pay her rather than doing it just out of despite (as it appeared).

There are way too many facts here for me not to believe that Bill has done a number on this family. My dad and mom, Duane, Joe, their wives, Janece, and Don know this to be the truth and have stood firmly knowing he has done wrong to their mother. We will not be a part of abuse to Mom. Whenever a person chooses to look away, that person is just as guilty as the person who does it. Don and Janece, Duane, Joe, and their wives have tried to get Bill to be accountable for what he has done. The other seven believe they are making their mother's last days as happy as they can be by looking the other way. They don't realize Grandma really wanted their help in controlling Bill and his abuse to her She really was not happy with her family not supporting each other I hope everyone can live with themselves if this truth is ever made known. You told me over the phone that you would be extremely upset if you found out that Bill verbally abused Grandma. I'm sending this to you because I want you to be aware. Please make phone calls and find out for yourself. I know that if you ask Grandma herself, she will tell you it's not true (that's what the abusee does because they don't want to go through abuse again). Bill has beaten her down way too many times for her to come clean. You can take this information and do whatever you want with it. If you choose not to believe any of this information and do not try to find out anyone else's side of the story, then I hope you will be able to live with your choice.

I know my dad tried for all these years to be his mother's best friend and to help her understand how wrong all this was. It hurts me so much that these seven have made up their mind to make their mother happy and not even try to come and visit their dying brother.

Diane

I will stay with Ken's life for a while.

Ken, his wife, Joe, his wife, Pete and his wife, Janece, and I planned a trip to Branson, Missouri. Duane and wife were to go also, but had some words with Pete and his wife and decided not to go. We spent a couple of days taking in shows. Ken was really lost when it came to shows. The shows really confused him, and all he wanted to do was play golf. When we left Branson, Ken, Joe, and wife came home to our house because we had made an appointment with our lawyer to try to get ahold of what our rights were as a family member on the land matter.

Janece and I would go to Ken's in Omaha, Nebraska at least two times a month. Some of the time I was playing a slow pitch softball tournament, and other times we just wanted to be with him. We knew his time was limited and did not want to have any if onlys. We did spend at least two days a month with them. They made all the games with us. Ken got to know all the players, kept up with all the scores, knew what the next field we would play on, and gave all the players a high five after each game even though he could not talk anymore in sentences. He found away to tell us. He was remarkable. After we finished our games, we went to their favorite place for our dinner, go to their home, and play 500. If Ken was your partner, you had a good chance of winning. His kids made up an 8 by 10 paper with numbers and suits because he could not speak He or we would just point to the bid we wanted. He did very well.

The next year was really tough. The "wonderful or maybe the magnificent seven" never came to visit Kenny. They knew the shape he was in because Ken's daughter had sent a letter by e-mail to all the brothers, sisters, plus Mom in June of 2010. She told us that her father, Kenny, had been diagnosed with frontotemporal dementia, which is a very rare form of dementia. The doctors told them he needed to get all his business in order because this could go very last. She told us, *if you want to see your brother when he will still know you and be able to visit with you, you better come soon because he doesn't have that much time.* (Kenny died in December 2011.

That summer before Ken died, the *"wonderful or magnificent seven"* *came* to Lone Rock to celebrate Mom's 100th birthday even though she would not be 100 until December. Ken's son and family were even planning to take him, but when they came to get him, he said, "No, no," and would not go. The "wonderful or magnificent seven" were there. You would think they would go to visit Ken in Omaha. They were only two and a half hours away from him. It was just out of their way. I found out later that some of them went to Alaska for a week or so instead of visiting their dying brother. Later, Bud called and wanted to come and visit Ken. He said he was just in the area—Montezuma, Iowa. Three and a half hours away??? *In the ared*?? Ken did not have a clue who he was. He did give him a hug, but that is what he did to everyone he met. After Bud left, Ken never indicated he knew who he was. Janece and I went to visit about two weeks later, and Ken handed Janece a piece of paper with Bud's name written on it. Janece looked at Ken, and he just shrugged his shoulders and held up his hands like he did not have a clue who that was. Kenny's wife was surprised about that because he had not indicated anything about Bud since he had been there. We do not know what Ken was really trying to tell us. Then, Dale called a couple weeks later that he was in the area and wanted to come and see Ken. Ken really did not know who he was. They gave Ken a Snap-on tool something. Ken did not know what it was for. Ken had been in the Snap-on tool business for over thirty years and did not remember what it was. Ken just gave it to his grandchildren. If they would have listened to Dianes emails to the whole family in the beginning of Ken's illness and come to visit, he would have known all of them and felt their support.

They choose not to, and then only two of them chose to come when it was too late. So sad.

The letters listed below were from Ken's daughter to the family from the beginning, sharing with them *Ken's condition* and a letter to a cousin trying to get support from her.

Hi, Janece! Thanks again for your call last night. It was good to talk to you. I've talked to Duane and his wife, and missed a call from Joe's wife. I sure appreciate everyone's support!

Duane's wife said something about Frank, Grandma's neighbor in Texas. He has heard Bill yell ar Grandma numerous times and would testify about that. I'm wondering if somehow I can get through to Ann to say that there is some proof that Grandma has been verbally abused and that she might be the key person in this family to possibly make things change. Ann told me that if she ever found out that Bill verbally abused Grandma, she would be very upset and would not let that happen. I'm wondering if Bud has been truthful with his daughter, Ann. She did tell me that Bud asked his mother if there was anything she needed to tell him. They all don't think Grandma would ever lie to them, but they don't understand that if someone is being verbally abused, they will lie to protect their abuser. Anyway, is Frank still your neighbor? Would he be willing to talk to Ann? If so, I'd like to either give Ann his phone number or have her talk to him if she comes to visit Bud, her father, in the park. If she would investigate a little more, maybe she would find the truth.

Ann,

If you axe having a hard time with Bill's abuse to Emma, you could call Bill's daughter and ask her why she left home at sixteen and never came back.

I know there was abuse there because of what her ex-mother-in-law told Janece, because they were friends even though Janece was not married anymore to her brother. Bill's daughter told her about her father's (Bill) abuse to her and her mother.

Just want you to have as much information.

Let me know what you think.

Diane

P.S. I also sent Ann a copy of the letter from Frank (neighbor in Texas) and the deed of land sale to Don's ex-wife so she has physical proof.

I was told by Frank, our neighbor, later that Bud and Dale called him on the day when they were both there and asked if they could come and see him. He told them that they could. When they got there, they asked about what he had seen of Bill and Mom in the past years and if it was true. Frank told them it sure was and he would go to court and tell it if he needed to. The two of them left and never said anything about it again. And after that, Mom would say she didn't like her neighbor Frank I know better than that, because Frank did so much for her and protected her just like she was his own sister. This also told me when it came to Ann going to make sure Bill was not abusing Mom. She had said something to her father, Bud and he told her to stay out of it, or something like that.

We took Dad back to the *med* center for a swallowing test on Monday. Mom and I could actually watch what the doctor was giving him go down his throat with the special X-ray machine that they had. When he drinks liquids, not everything goes down where it is supposed to—some of it is going into his lungs. She gave him things of different consistencies, and it showed that foods such as pudding, applesauce, Jell-O, and malts go down easier for him.

He can no longer talk at all anymore and cannot comprehend what we say so communication is extremely difficult. He sometimes writes a word on paper, and sometimes it makes sense and sometimes it doesn't. He's lost about fifty pounds and is very frail. So far he usually has a smile on his face and always gives people big hugs when they come. Don and Janece have been coming once a month and he is always glad to see them. Duane, his wife, and daughter came just this past Monday and hope to come once a month to visit also. Joe and wife hope to come soon. I appreciate those who have given us so much support. It is greatly appreciated, and I know Dad appreciates it too. As fast as he is declining, I hope those that don't even attempt to come and see him will be able to live with that decision. He is a great father, brother, and son, and I hope you all realize how special he is and can tell him that, and support his own family that is dealing with all of this pain. It is so hard going through this as his daughter, knowing how divided this family is and not getting the support and love that he and we could really use right now. I know you all think of him and pray for him, but when you don't make an effort to come see him and do not show any support to my mother, it is hard for me to take.

All of his troubles started getting worse when Grandma hung up that phone on him, and I really have a hard time with that. I don't know that I can ever forgive her for not apologizing to him when we told her how hurt Dad was when she did that to him, when we've written her letters asking her to do so, and how some of this family can view us as hateful to have sent those letters to Grandma. This is *not* about Grandma—it is about my dad and your brother. When he could talk awhile back, he said a few times that his mother is dead, so what does that tell you?????
I am sending each of you what I sent to Ann. I didn't have her email address, so I mailed it to her home address last Friday (24th). We'll see if she does anything with this information. Thanks for all of your support. I appreciate it! Diane.

Keep in touch. Let us know how it goes.

We saw a specialized ALS doctor this afternoon since the EMG test he had done a few weeks ago came back abnormal. This doctor did some more testing on Dad's muscles, and clinically speaking it does look like he has ALS. They say that with the frontotemporal dementia that he has been diagnosed with, 10 percent of those people develop symptoms of ALS. Unfortunately, it looks like we are falling into that 10 percent. We'll go back in September for a three-hour consultation with the doctor, speech pathologist, case worker, physical therapist, and I can't remember who else. Sounds like about six different people will be talking with us and examining Dad.

Dad was also told us that he could no longer drive this past Monday when we took him to the rehab center where they tested him. Unfortunately, he cannot comprehend much of what is being asked of him, so it is no longer safe to let him drive. He was quite angry, and I don't blame him. It doesn't seem fair that things keep getting taken away from him, and I don't know if he fully comprehends what is going on with his mind and body. It is definitely hard for all of us to watch.

Please continue to keep all of us in your prayers.

I wanted to update the family on Dad's health. We saw a neurologist a few weeks ago, and he told us that Dad looks like he is developing the first signs of ALS as he is beginning to have twitches in his arms, legs, and tongue that he cannot control. When we got the dementia diagnosis last June, the doctor did indicate that with this rare form of dementia (frontotemporal dementia), he could develop symptoms similar to ALS or Parkinson's disease. We go in for an EMG (test where they check his nerves and muscles) on May 6, which will verify whether or not he has ALS too.

Dan, Chris, and their family will be bringing Dad to Grandma's party in June if he is up for the drive. For those of you that don't feel you would be welcomed to come and see Dad, you are terribly mistaken. (Don and Janece, Duane and Paula, Pete and wife have all come, and Joe and wife are coming next month). Mom has only said that she did not feel comfortable talking on the phone as she gets quite emotional, but she has never indicated that anyone could not come to visit. It is difficult for him to visit as he can only say a few words here and there, but so far Mom is pretty good about filling in the blanks.

All along, all Mom and I wanted to do was to let Grandma know how much she hurt Dad when she hung up the phone on him, and was hoping that she could apologize for doing that and let him know how much she loves him. We have expressed this to her, but evidently our letters have been viewed as hateful. She told my mom in her birthday card that my mom must not think that Grandma cares about Dad, and that she would like to see him but can't. Obviously, people have been telling her that no one is allowed to visit Dad. She still has yet to apologize for hanging up the phone on him. That is the last memory Dad has of her and Mom, and I only want Dad to have a happy memory of her, not a hurtful one. She has no idea what we are going through.

Please keep our family in your prayers. This has been tremendously hard on all of us, especially for my mom as she is with my dad all the time. She could use your prayers and support the most as this is only going to get harder. She and I are not hateful people—we've always faithfully sent Grandma cards and visited her as much as possible. We care a lot, and it has been hurtful that people could think otherwise.

I will keep you posted of any other health updates.

Diane

I am sending each of you what I sent to Ann. I didn't have her email address, so I mailed it to her home address last Friday (24th). We'll see if she does anything with this information. Thanks for all of your support. I appreciate it! Thanks, Kathy, for the copies of emails. I received them in the mail today. Thanks for keeping me informed.

P.S. I also sent a copy of the letter from Frank (neighbor in Texas) and the deed of land sale to Irene so she has physical proof. Thank you.

Diane

We brothers supporting Ken and his family got this email from Ken's daughter:

We are putting Dad into a very nice assisted living memory care unit here in Omaha on Sunday, November 6. This will be very difficult for Dan, Mom, and myself, but we know it is time as he has gotten much weaker, is down to 137 pounds, and his swallowing has become much more difficult as he eats. He hasn't been able to talk for a while and now he no longer comprehends, so communication is extremely difficult. The doctor explained it to us that he hears voices, but it is like being in a foreign country where you don't know the language.

The address to Brighton Gardens is 9220 Western Avenue, Suite 134, Omaha, NE 68114. He will not haw a phone in his room as he cannot talk and he will not have a mailbox. If you want to send anything you can, send it to the home address, or if you want to send it to Brighton Gardens, they will leave it for Mom to pick up.

I don't know how many times I have told everyone how our family feels, and it's frustrating when I hear that we don't understand the other side of the family's story. There is no other side. The fact is that Grandma hung up the phone on my dad. I don't think anyone except my mom knows how bad that hurt my dad and what it did to him. Part of him died that day. I've had it with people saying such mean things about my mother. She sent the letters to Grandma to try to get her to understand what she did and all the hurt feelings that she caused. I would think if anyone was in my mom's shoes that they would have done the same, knowing how bad someone hurt their spouse When we wrote to Grandma asking her to apologize so that Dad could have a happy memory of her and she refused to do so, she has no idea the hurt and bitter feelings she has caused on this end. Everyone has known my mom for many years and knows all the kind things that she has done throughout those years, but yet you can snap your finger, judge her, and say cruel things about her. I just don't get it and am tired of some of the family not supporting her. You say you are defending your mom, so are you defending her for hanging up the phone on your brother and crushing him? It sure would be nice to have a family that sent love and support to the caregivers of their brother and son during his last months with us. The neurologist said he probably has 1–2 years left, his primary doctor said one year, but I think this will be our last Christmas with him and it is just a matter of time before we lose him. I don't think you realize how bad some of you have hurt Dan, my mom, and myself by not giving us the support that you would think family would give during this difficult time I think for me I am done with my emails to those of you that have not shown much support. If you want to see him, you can come and visit him at Brighton Gardens, but know that he may or may not know you, and will not be able to speak or understand anything that you say. I was hoping some of you could see him before he got this way as I think now it might be too late.

Diane

Honoring My Brother Kenny's life HONORING HIS LIFE

GOD'S GARDEN

God looked around his garden And found an empty place.
He then looked down upon the earth And saw your tired face.
He put his arms around you And lifted you to rest.
God's garden must be beautiful He always takes the best.

He saw the road was getting rough And the hills were hard to climb, So he closed your weary eyelids And whispered, "Peace be thine." It broke our hearts to lose you But you didn't go alone, For part of us went with you The day God called you home.

PRAYER
Pastor Ken Wittrock

TRIBUTES
Bob Friend
Janece Hutchinson

READING (Janece Hutchinson) Life is but a stepping place, A pause in what's to be, A resting place along the road, To sweet eternity. We all have different journeys, Different paths along the way,

We all were meant to learn some things,
But never meant to stay… Our destination is a place, Far greater than we know, For some the journey's quicker, For some the journey's slow.
And when the journey finally ends,
We ll claim a great reward,
And find an everlasting peace, Together with the Lord.

BLESSING
Pastor Ken Wittrock

KEN HUTCHINSON

Saturday, December 10, 2011 11:00 AM.
Rejoice! Lutheran Church

The people that were there were the most caring people I have been around. Well-dressed and caring, just a bunch of caring people that were the best. With all the brothers and sisters, a person would think there would have had more than brother Duane and wife along with myself and Janece. We flew in from Texas, and Duane drove in from Garner, Iowa.

Janece and I cherish the times we spent with my brother, Kenny.

The following is the last letter Kenny's daughter sent to two of the brothers she felt caused the family destruction.

Bud & Dale,

I told myself I wasn't going to send anymore emails to you, but I just have to get some things off my chest. I am so disappointed that you two allowed Grandma's will to be changed. I remember Dad telling me that he was so upset about Grandma hanging up that phone on him and telling him that she was going to take him out of the will. I remember Mom telling me that Dad talked to Dale shordy after that had happened, and that Dale reassured Dad not to worry and that and he'd talk to Grandma. This all happened around the time that the will was indeed changed in 2010. Dad was diagnosed with frontotemporal dementia in June of 2010, and then after Grandma hung up on him and crushed him, things progressed downhill pretty quickly for Dad. That is the same year I sent out my famous letter to everyone telling them I just wish everyone could come together and support our family. Instead, everyone couldn't get past the letters Mom wrote to Grandma trying to tell her how bad she hurt my dad. It was also hurtful for me to have Ann call me and tell me that she couldn't believe I could do that to Grandma. That letter had nothing to do about Grandma. It was about Dad! I also sent letters to Grandma trying to tell her that she needed to apologize to Dad and help Dad have a happy memory of her instead of a hurtful one, but she chose not to do that. I was never able to forgive her for not doing that. I don't think anyone realizes what she did to my dad's spirit. I am still unable to forgive all those who said terrible things about my mom and showed her no support at all during those difficult two years before Dad was gone. People couldn't believe that Mom sent your sympathy cards back to you when he passed. Bud's wife made it a point to tell me that Mom sent her card back. I guess I have a hard time understanding how you couldn't get that she did do that. I certainly don't blame her!!! You show sympathy when it's too late???

Also, Dad did not understand why you two came to visit him the summer before he passed. He wrote your names down on a piece of paper and then shrugged his shoulders and looked puzzled. I still can't understand why no one even tried to come and see him sooner, especially after I had told everyone his diagnosis a while ago.

I am also disappointed that Dan and I never got a copy of Grandma's will since we are entitled to what was to be Dad's. Our names and addresses were given along with Duane, Don, and Joe, so the lawyer did have our information. Joe's wife had to call the lawyer and make sure we got copies. We only got our copies today after everyone else got theirs last week or even earlier. I don't expect much because I am sure there have been dealings over these last few years that would make sure that the four of us would not get much. My dad was all about things being fair and I am too, but I don't think this family knows what fair is.

One last thing. I was so disappointed when Bud sent the list out of what everyone was to get of Grandma's. Why would you list what only some of the grandkids were to get? Why would you want everyone to know that Amy was to get Grandma's ring? How do you think that makes the rest of the grandkids feel????

I blame the two of you for a lot of this family mess. I thought originally you wanted to make sure this family would be united, but I fear that money showed you a different way to think Like I said, Dad always wanted things fair, and that's whar I want too. Please make sure Dan and I are entitled to whatever was to go to our dad. That's the least you can do for us.

—Diane

I'm writing this book with a prayer that the information I am sharing will help other families from having to go through the heartbreak we have gone through with our family. Our family shows the truth of the statement… "Money is the root of all evil."

I guess it is time to get back to the serious part of the book Janece and I went to the courthouse in Algona, Iowa, did some research on the forty acres that was in question, had some copies made, and took them to a lawyer. He looked them over and could not believe I did not know that this land *had been* mine with brothers and mates for the last thirty years. I was always told it was like Dad's land, which was a life estate until Mom passed, then we kids owned it. So I thought I had no reason to question what I thought was farmed by Bill and shared with Mom. Then finding out that someone was getting what I was supposed to have a say to and that it has been going on for the last thirty years, I knew I needed to look into more happenings of the farm and my mother. *What happened to the income and expense record for that thirty years—got the subsides, who paid for what, did Mom get paid correctly?*

For what it's worth, some people may fine this interesting but then again.

Below I hate listed the actions that went on with Mom and land that I knew nothing about, because I trusted that my older brother would not do wrong to his mother and other family members.

The following is what I found, which took my brother Duane and myself to take action to find out the facts.

My Family
(Information found at Recorders Office Kossuth Court House)

August 10, 1971—Warranty Deed—XXXXXX, husband of XXXXXX— in consideration of the sum of ONE DOLLAR ($1.00) and other good and valuable consideration in hand paid do hereby convey unto XXXXXXX—Kossuth County, Iowa to wit:—The East One Half (E1/2) of The South One Half (S1/2) of Section One (1), Township Ninety-Seven (97) North, Range Thirty (30), West of the 5th P.M.—(This purpose of this deed is to sever a joint tenancy ownership and the consideration for same is less than $ 1,000.00 and does not require revenue stamps.)

(Book 105, page 129)

July 25, 1975—Real Estate Contract for SE1/4-SW1/4 of Section One—Bill for $50,000—Book 173, at page 252 of the records of the Kossuth County Recorder

**Accountability requested—What was the amount of the down payment *and* conditions of the contract? Show proof of contract and payments.

December 24, 1979—My Father Passes

**Accountability request—Who is the trustee of the life estate? And who makes the decisions? Has this life estate required a K1 & 1041 forms be sent in yearly with tax return? Why or why not? We understand we kids have ownership of this life estate at the time of Mom's death, and we understand we should have been receiving yearly statements. We have not seen a statement yet year to date and are asking for these statements. We have been told a "set aside wetland" has been added to these acres also and question why we were not consulted on this decision since this required a contract for a few years that could involve us if Mom would pass during the contract. Why were we not consulted?

December 28, 1979—Absolute Gift

An absolute gift to each child and their mates (names on deed) South One Half of the Southeast Quarter of the Southeast Quarter (Sl/2 SE1/4 SE1/4) of Section One (1) Township Ninety-Seven (97) North, Range Thirty (30) West of the 5th P.M. This deed constitutes an absolute gift to the children and spouses of grantor's children, and revenue stamps are not required and the transfer is exempt from valuation sheet. Why didn't each one of us get a copy of this absolute gift at the time??

March 5, 1980—An absolute gift to each child and their mates (names on deed)

North One Half of the Southeast Quarter of the Southeast Quarter (N1/2 SE1/4) of Section One (1) Township Ninety-Seven (97) North, Range Thirty (30 West ofthe 5th P.M.) This deed constitutes an absolute gift to the children and spouses of grantor's children and revenue stamps are not required, and this deed constitutes an absolute gift to the children and spouses of grantor's children, and revenue stamps are not required and the transfer is exempt from valuation sheet. (Book 122, page 340) (Question on this: Who received the income on this after Bill XXX brought from Duane XXX, Joe XXX, Sue XXX, and Joan XXXX???) (With both absolute gift deeds, each couple owned undivided 3.48 Acres or 1/11th or 1.74 Acres or 1/22nd.)

**Accountability needed—We were absolute owners since 1979/80 and have not been consulted on anything. (We did not understand we were owners. We were told it was like the life estate and did not question until we became aware of other unfair happenings. which began our checking things out.) We need accountability on *all* activities of these past years. And do not come back and tell us that we agreed on giving all incomes to Mom's. We did not agree to this or was even asked. I received a CCC-509 form with my signature on it that was not my signature (dated 2009; I was not the person that signed this form). How many times did someone else sign my name without my authorization? This is call fraud! Government subsidies have been involved. Show who has been receiving these and how owners were not consulted.

March 20, 1981—Federal Estate Tax Lien—$34,824.00—SW1/4 of Section 1 Township 97 North, Range 30, West of the 5th P.M. Except the SE1/4 thereof: in Kossuth County, IA. Book 4, Page 445

**Accountability needed—(Where did this tax lien come from?? Is this Bill's XXXX since he started buying this July 25, 1975, or is this part of Dad's estate taxes???) If it was part of Dad's estate, why was it not paid as stated in his will—Item I—"I direct that all of my just debts, including expenses of last illness, burial, and cost of administering this my last will and testament, be first paid out of my estate."

May 1, 1981—Joint Tenancy Warranty Deed from Joe XXXX and wife to Bill XXX and wife—1/11 interest in and to the real estate described as: Southeast Quarter of the Southeast Quarter (SE1/4 SE1/4) Township

Ninety-Seven (97) North, Range Thirty (30) West of the 5th P.M. (Sept. 27, 1999 was not recorded until this date Book 1999, page 3289)

January 10, 1995—Federal Estate Tax Lien—$34,824.00 Released (Book 2 page, US Liens.)

    ** Accountability needed—Who paid this? How was this paid off?) (Fourteen years later!) Why so long in paying? If Bill had enough money to buy acres from two other farmers in his area in 1994, why would he or Mom not have enough money to pay off this lien earlier?

January 26, 1998—Real estate contract dated July 25, 1975 paid in completion—Book 160 ld—Page 214 (Twenty-three years later)

May 16, 1999—Joint tenancy warranty deed from Duane XXXX and wife to Bill XXXX and wife—1/11 interest in and to the real estate described as: Southwest Quarter of Section 1, Township 97 North, Range 30, West of the 5th P.M. Kossuth County, Iowa, *except* the Southeast Quarter thereof.—Consideration less than $500, therefore, decoration of value and groundwater hazard statement not required. (Jan. 5, 2000 it was changed to *and* February 2nd, 2002 corrected paperwork in it, and recorded.)

Oct. 30, 2002—Real Estate Contract (Short Form)—Mom, a single person, to Bill XXXX and ED XXXX—The West Half of the Southeast Quarter (Wl/2 SE1/4) and the Northeast Quarter of the Southeast (Quarter NE1/4 SE1/4) all in Section One (1) Township Ninety-Seven (97) North Range Thirty (30) West of the 5th P.M. Kossuth County, IA. For $202,986.00 of which $15,000 has been paid—$15,000 on Jan. 2, 2003, $7,362.39 on July 1, 2003, $7,362.39 on Jan 2, 2004, and a like amount on each July 1st and January 2nd each year thereafter until July 1, 2023, at which time the unpaid balance shall become due and payable— at a 6 percent interest per annum included payable semiannually, & included in above payment installment of real estate taxes becoming due and payable October 1, 2003 by seller—Mom—possession at closing. The parties acknowledge the law firm of XXXX & XXXX is representing *only the buyers* in connection with this transaction.

***Accountability needed—On the contract, it states they were not representing Mom, only the buyer. Why would she not have representation to protect her best interests?

Jan. 25, 2005—Warranty deed from Sue XXXX, a single person, to Bill XXX an undivided 1/11 interested in the Southeast Quarter of the Southeast Quarter (SE1/4 SE1/4) of Section One (1) Township Ninety-Seven (97) North, Range Thirty (30) West of the 5th P.M. Kossuth County IA. (May 2, 2005 was recorded in the courthouse.)

Jan. 9, 2007—Warranty deed from Joan XXX and husband, wife & husband to Bill XXX and undivided 1/11 interest in—Southeast Quarter of the Southeast Quarter (SE1/4 SE¼) of Section One (1) Township Ninety-Seven (97) North, Range Thirty (30) West of the 5th P.M. Kossuth County, IA. (Jan. 24, 2007 was recorded in the courthouse.)

Nov. 12, 2007—Statement of Escrow Agent—The undersigned states that there was deposited with the undersigned, as escrow agent, within the 180 days last past and instrument of conveyance concerning real estate situation in Kossuth County, IA in which Mom is grantor and Bill XXXX & Ed XXXX is grantee—Signed on October 30, 2002.

**Accountability needed—Why was this just recorded Nov. 2007 and not October 30, 2002 when the contract was established?

Feb. 8, 2007—Bill XXXX—presents a letter to the rest of the kids in family information on an examined abstract of tide, in one part covering the following described real estate, to wit—the South Half (S1/2) of Section One (1) Township Ninety-Seven (97) North, Range Thirty (30) West of the 5th P.M. Kossuth County, IA. Etc. (On page 3 of letter)

**Nothing was answered through this letter. It was just words.

Feb. 21, 2007—Warranty *deed* for the consideration of $100 & other valuable consideration. Mom, a single person, do hereby convey to Bill XXXX & ED XXXX the following real estate—The West Half of the Southeast Quarter (W1/2 SE1/4) and the Northeast Quarter of the Southeast Quarter (NE1/4 SE1/4 all in Section One (1) Township Ninety-Seven (97) North, Range Thirty (30) West of the 5ᵗʰ P.M. Kossuth County, IA. (October 30, 2002 was when this contract began—Document No 4722—$150,000.00 was the amount paid in full to put closure to the contract.)

Feb. 12, 2007—Open-End Real Estate Mortgage—Security State Bank-Bill & wife XXXX & ED & wife XXXX for $75,000.00 *per* Couple.

Feb. 25, 2007—Bill XXXX presented family with a copy of his amortization schedule he was to be following to make payments to Mom on contract. It really is showing correct payment of principle and interest were made. We have asked for a copy of the checks front and back. We are to be seen them around the 10ᵗʰ of March. (Pre—Bud XXXX) This *never happened*!!

**Accountability needed—This was not clear at all. We want proof of checks showing payments with interest.

March 23, 2009—Security State Bank, Algona IA—Release of Real Estate Mortgage—Book 2009—Page 1856—On the 20ᵗʰ day of February, AD. 2007, is redeemed, paid off, satisfied, and discharged in full. (This was the $75,000.00 loan *per* couple—Document No 4722 total together $150,000.00. Book 2007, page 774)

December 18, 2009—Warranty Deed—For the consideration of $0 dollars and other valuable consideration, Bill and wife XXXX, husband and wife, convey to Ed XXXX, subject to the life estate of each Bill XXXX and wife XXXX the following described real estate in Kossuth County, IA.—The Southeast Quarter of the Southwest Quarter (SE ¼ SW 1/4) of the Section One (1), Township NinetySeven (97) North, Range Thirty (30) West of the 5th P.M., Kossuth County, IA. (This is a transfer between parents and son without consideration; neither declaration of value, groundwater hazard statement, nor transfer taxis required.)—Book 2009—Page 4909—Document 2009 4909

August 22, 2010—Real Estate Contract—Short Form—Grantees—Bill XXXX—Grantors—Dale XXXX & wife XXX-#410- 13-01-400-004; Document 2010 2517 Book 2010 Page 2517 type Contr Pg 5 Date 8/19/2010—Rec Amt $29.00 And Amt—$5.00—DOV # 290—AN UNDIVIDED 1/11 INTEREST IN: THE SOUTHEAST QUARTER OF THE SOUTHEAST QUARTER (SE ¼ SE ¼) OF SECTION ONE (1) TOWNSHIP NINETYSEVEN (97) NORTH, RANGE THIRTY (30) WEST OF THE 5TH P.M., KOSSUTH COUNTY, IOWA— TWELVE THOUSAND SEVEN HUNDRED EIGHTY-NINE AND 0/100—THE UNPAID BALANCE, PRINCIPAL AND INTEREST, SHALL BECOME DUE AND PAYABLE ON AUGUST 2015. INTEREST BUYERS SHALL PAY INTEREST FROM AUGUST 15, 2015

ON THE UNPAID BALANCE OF THE RATE OF 5 PERCENT PER ANNUM, PAYABLE ANNUALLY ON AUG. 15. SELLER SHALL GIVE BUYERS POSSESSION OF THE REAL ESTATE ON AUGUST 15, 2010 PROVIDED BUYERS ARE NOT IN DEFAULT UNDER THIS CONTRACT. CLOSING SHALL BE ON AUGUST 15, 2010

August 23, 2010—Warranty Deed Grantees: Ed XXX; Grantors: Pete XXXX & wife XXXX—#910-13-01400-004 Amber Garman, 07 County Auditor—Document 2010 2518; Book 2010 Pg 2518—Type WD Pg

2.—Date 8/19/2010—Rec Amt $14.00 and Amt $5.00 Rev Transfer Tax $20.00—Rev Stamp # 290—DOV # 291—AN UNDIVIDED 1/11ᵀᴴ INTEREST IN—THE SOUTHEAST QUARTER OF THE SOUTH-EAST QUARTER) SE ¼ SE ¼ OF SECTION ONE (1) TOWNSHIP NINETYSEVEN (97) NORTH, RANGE THIRTY (30), WEST OF THE 5ᵀᴴ P.M., KOSSUTH COUNTY, IOWA (CHECK WAS TO BE $ 12,789.00 TO PAY IN FULL)

August 23, 2010—Warranty Deed—Grantees: Bill XXXX—Grantors: Fred XXXX & wife XXXXXX—# 910-13-01-400-004—Document 2010—2516 Book 2010 Page 2516—Type WD Pg 2—Date 8/19/2010—Rec Amt $14.00 Aud. Amt $5.00 Rev. Transfer Tax $20.00—Rev. Stamp # 289—DOV #289—AN UNDIVIDED 1/11ᵀᴴ INTEREST IN: THE SOUTHEAST QUARTER OF THE SOUTHEAST QUARTER (SE ¼ SE 1/4) OF SECTION ONE (1), TOWNSHIP NINETY-SEVEN (97) NORTH, RANGE THIRTY (30), WEST OF THE 5ᵀᴴ P.M., KOSSUTH COUNTY, IOWA (CHECK WAS TO BE $12,789.00 TO PAY IN FULL)

August 23, 2010—Real Estate Contract—Short Form—Grantees: ED XXXX—Grantors: Bud XXXX & wife XXXX—August 23, 2010—#910-13-01-400-004—Document 2010 2519 Book 2010 Pg 2519 Type Contr—Date 8/19/2010—Rec. Amt $29.00—Aud Amt $5.00 DOV #292—AN UNDIVIDED 1/11 INTEREST IN: THE SOUTHEAST QUARTER OF THE SOUTHEAST
QUARTER (SE ¼ SE ¼) OF SECTION ONE (1), TOWNSHIP NINETY-SEVEN (97) NORTH, RANGE THIRTY (30), WEST OF THE 5ᵀᴴ P.M., KOSSUTH COUNTY, IOWA.—TOTAL PURCHASE PRICE OF THE REAL ESTATE IS—TWELVE THOUSAND SEVEN HUNDRED EIGHTY-NINE AND 0/100 ($12,789.00)—INTER-EST—BUYERS SHALL PAY INTEREST FROM AUG. 15, 2010 ON

THE UNPAID BALANCE AT RAT OF 5 PERCENT ANNUM PAYABLE—ANNUALLY ON AUGUST 15TH. SELLERS SHALL GIVE BUYERS POSSESSION OF THE REAL ESATE ON AUGUST 15, 2010 PROVIDED BUYERS ARE NOT IN DEFAULT.

October 27, 2010—WARRANTY DEED—Grantees: Ed XXXX—Grantors: Don's ex-wife (Don Hutchinson's ex-wife, which Don was working on with another lawyer in getting her name off the 1/11th. Don did not know of this absolute gift at the time of his divorce, so did not have it written in that she had to sign off. Ed knew Don was working at getting her name off!!) Document 2010 3401 Book 2010 Pg 3401 Type WD Pg 1—Date 10/27/1010 Rec Amt $9.00 Aud Amt $5.00 Rev Trans for Tax $9.60. Rev Stamp # 380—DOV # 389 AN INDIVIDED 1/22ND INTEREST IN: THE SOUTHEAST QUARTER OF THE SOUTHEAST QUARTER (SE ¼ SE ¼) OF SECTION ONE (1), TOWNSHIP NINETYSEVEN (97) NORTH, RANGE THIRTY (30), WEST OF THE 5TH P.M., KOSSUTH COUNTY, IOWA. (THE CHECK MUST HAVE BEEN ABOUT $6,500.00 ACCORDING TO THE REV. STAMPS.)

JANUARY 19, 2011—WARRANTY DEED—Grantees: Ed XXX—Grantors: Bud XXXX n & wife XXXX—AN UNDIVIDED 1/11TH INTEREST IN: THE SOUTHEAST QUARTER OF THE SOUTHEAST QUARTER (SE ¼ SE ¼) OF SECTION ONE (1), TOWNSHIP NINETY-SEVEN (97) NORTH, RANGE THIRTY (30), WEST OF THE 5TH P.M., KOSSUTH COUNTY, IOWA.

April 12, 2011—Warranty Deed—Grantees: Ed XXX—Grantors: Don XXX—Undivided 1/22 interest for Dons interest. The SE1/4 of SE1/4 of Section One Township (79), Range 30, West of the 5th P.M. Kossuth County IA Book 2011 Pg 1126

April 12, 2011—Warranty Deed—Grantees ED XXX—Grantors Ken & wife XXX—Undivided 1/22 interest of each party. The SE ¼ of SE1/4 of Section One Township (79) Range 30, West of 5th P.M. Kossuth County, IA. Book 2011 Pg 1125

Through all of this, I have found out so muck I encourage all families to know what is going on with their folks' estates and help their folks altogether as a family to keep a family from being destroyed at the time of parents' death. Our family is such a sad, sad happening. I pray, through sharing my experience, that I can help other family from this heartbreak.

My wife and I went through a court to try to get the income I was cheated out of, with proof of paperwork and everything from the acres I did not know I was shared owner of. I lost that case because the judge said, yes, Bill had done everything wrong, but I had waited too long to report it. Even when I told the judge that I came forward as soon as I found out, he would not accept it. A good lawyer friend, Jim Hicks from Knoxville, IA, said, "You just got *homered*"! That means the judge rules in favor of the hometown lawyers.

My brother Duane and I went to court to get the income Bill had cheated our morn out of by what Bill called sharecropping, then it somehow turned into rent or whatever Bill wanted it to be called. Bill had always taken the corn profit, and Mom got the beans profit. We had again all the paperwork, from co-ops, bank statements, etc., showing the unfairness of it and what Mom should have gotten. Again, the judge ruling was, yes, Bill, did wrong, but still rules in Bill's favor. Again, our lawyer friend, Jim Hicks, shook his head and said, "So sad, you got *homered again*." My brother Duane figured out that if Mom had rented her land out all these years instead of sharecropping with brother Bill, she would have received over a million dollars and still own the land.

Sorry to say that this matter has sure made me question our trust in the judicial system that is supposed to protect us. I still know today that my mother really wanted Janece and I to help her when she said three times to Janece, "I have done something I should not have, but I will be gone by the time the rest of the kids find out." When anyone says something like that three times, the)' are crying out for help. And Janece and I were always there for Mom when she needed something. After Janece's mom passed, we became that much closer. The one joy and blessing we can say we have but the rest of the family will not ever be able to say is, we had nine wonderful years with both of our moms together, and then after Janece's mom passed, we had seventeen more years enjoying Mom before all the family mess came alive. Janece now would sure like to talk to her mom again and ask her more about what she meant in February 1989 and what she was trying to tell her when she said, "Don's mom is going to have a very sad happening with her family before she passes," and what her mother had said to her sister the same month, that, "Bill XXXX will never stay at my home again in Texas." What Janece feels is her mother experienced many happenings with Bill and his mother that her mother knew was not fair to the rest of the family. And her mother was hurting for her friend.

We are so blessed in our life to have our Lord guiding us and teaching us all the way. With his help, we found there is still life after heartbreak and hurts.

Today, I have some many accomplishments through it all. For the last few years, 2002 until now, I was busy playing… senior Olympics—football throw, first place every year, softball throw, first place every year, and softball throw for accuracy was not the best.

Janece and I have traveled a large part of the USA playing slow pitch ball with travel teams from the age bracket of sixty-five to now eighty years of age. We went to *Palm Springs CA, St George UT, Phoenix AZ, Las Vegas NV, Little Canada MN, Rochester MN, Mason City IA, Milwaukee WI, Troy IL, Columbus OH, Hot Springs AK, Tulsa OK, Houston TX, Austin TX, Cleveland OH, Lakeland FL, Ft Meyers FL, Shawnee KS, Liberty MO, Quad Cities IL.*

When I first started on my softball ventures, our Iowa senior team went to Louisville, KY to play with what we thought was a fair team of guys we put together. To our surprise, we came in first place. I was put on third base and never made an error. As a matter of fact, our umpire started calling me "Brooks." If I did a little research, I could come up with names like Ken Clark, Fred Bankus, and Norm Robinson. I know I could find all the names because Janece recorded all the games.

A little happening I remember was the Chicago team manager. After a loss to us, he took all the bats out of their dug out, put them on home plate, and started kicking them as far as he could. He did miss one bat. One of his teammates tossed the bat to him so he would get all the bats punished or whatever. We always have fun.

This was another good year, 2017. Our Buzzard team from Iowa qualified in first place to go to Birmingham, AL to play in the Wodd Series Senior Games. We took first place! I was not really on my game, but the rest of the team came through.

I did play shortstop—made a few good plays. I even got a compliment form Jake Wood (Jake was playing against us from another eighty-year-old team). He played for the Detroit Tigers years back When he came up to the plate, our outfielders went back to the 300 feet fence. He did bounce a couple off the fence, but all in vain. Score was Buzzards 12, Rivals 7. Buzzards really did not have a problem with the other teams. We had Tom Spear, Norm Robinson, Willie Fielderman, Stephen Agard, Fred Bankus Mgr, Larry Pardubsky, Don Stifel, Lynn Gibson, Bill Truesdale, and Bill Regynski.

We received this article by Bailley Freestone:

In June 12–14 two Dallas County residents traveled to Birmingham, AL to play the National Senior Games Championship softball tournament.

Adel resident Tom Spear, 76, and Don Stifel, 76, were part of a thirteen-man team: The Iowa Buzzards, which played in the 75 division. Spear began his ball in 2002. Teams came from over the country to the 75 plus division. There are 6 teams: Texas, Florida, Tennessee, New Jersey, Alabama, and of course *Iowa*. This isn't the Buzzards' first time. Since the founding of their team in 2014, they played annually in senior softball tournaments around the country with one goal in mind: to be competitive at the championships. The National championship are held every two years in a different city. In the senior games' thirty-year history, the Buzzards were the first Iowa team to come in first place in their division. (end of article)

When we had gone, we hadn't anticipated doing as well as we did because we were up against some really tough teams. I believe we played just about errorless games—maybe a few errors!!

Of the eight teams we played, two were against Tennessee, one and one. When the two teams had their playoff, the *Buzzards* came out first 13 to 9.

The Team Legends were led by former Detroit Tigers' Jake Wood, who played with them in the 1960s—nice guy.

We all played and enjoyed senior softball for a variety of reasons: stay in shape, fellowship, and hope for a longer life. The next Senior Games 2019 will be Albuquerque NM.

I have just celebrated my eighty-seoond birthday and still going strong, playing for KC Antiques from KC, Jimmy's from Minnesota, and of course *The Buzzards* from Iowa.

From Ball to a Face Lift—Just a little thing about my eyes

For some time, my eyes—lower lids—drooped. I went to a doctor in Des Moines. He made a cut under both eyes' comers to correct them. It worked for a while Yes, it *hurt! After* a while, they went back to where they were. So my doctor sent me up to see a doctor at Iowa City University Dr. Carter. When he saw me, he said I can see why you are here. They set me up for an operation for each eye. The procedure cut skin from the front of my left ear and placed it under my right eye. Then, they moved skin from my right ear to place it under my left eye Yes, it hurt!!!! No driving for a week. Janece was my driver for that week. When all this was happening, there were at least six students observing. One doctor cut skin from my ear and one sewed it to my eye. The one working on my ear had to pull the skin to cover the hole in front of my ear Not fun; I could feel some and see all that was going on. Went back a week later to have stitches removed; *not fun.* I did the eyes a month apart because I had to go to a ball tournament.

Well some time has passed since I have put the first part of my book together. Eyes are good. And then I took a tumble on July 25, 2018, running to first base. I tore all the tissues from my rotator cuff on my right shoulder I had surgery on August 1, 2018. Everything went fine.

I was kind of concerned for the pain I was supposed to have I had some pain, but not what everyone said was supposed to come from a rotator cuff operation.

My doctors and nurses took very good care of me. Top of the line group. Each group had their thing to do. They put an IV in my right hand; of course, it had a needle and a bag hanging on a pedestal with wheels. They opened a valve to let the fluid flow; whatever was in the tube was going in my body. I chose to have a nerve block to deaden my nerves in my shoulder. They told me they were going to put my right arm to sleep. I watched a screen—maybe 12 by 12. A guy was sticking a long needle in my nerve area, and moving the needle around in my nerve area. *Hurt, yes!* After a few injections, my arm started to get numb. I lay on table for some time. Next thing, I was put on another table, and pushed somewhere that was full of lights, a few people all dressed up in gowns and gloves, and lights in every place. I was placed on another table. Next thing, I heard was *ok, you can set up now.* It was a bit of struggle because it seemed like I had no right arm. At that time, I did not have any pain. I had to use my left hand to feel if my right hand was still there; it was there. It felt like someone else's arm. Later that night, some feeling came back. I took a pain pill in the morning and another one in the evening. My arm was in a sling. I was told, "*You have to have that on for six weeks.*" It was a little tough when it came to doing my duty. I had to have help in shower. Janece came to the shower, which was all the help I needed. After a week, I could do a good job of handling all things myself. We have a sleep number bed that helped me keep my top half up for sleeping. That did a fine job keeping me from roaming the house trying to get comfortable.

Week have gone by. A little stiff and only pains when I move a little too far I should be fine in another few days. I would like to put the sling away; they say I have to wear it another month. I will be ready to play ball by this winter in South Texas. This is my reward for having fun since I retired and started doing what I do best. God isn't finished with me yet, and I am so glad.

What got me this medal was Senior Softball throw. The first time was 197 feet; this year was only 157 feet in June 2018, which is first for my age group, eighty years. No one has passed that mark since I started in the Senior Olympics. 2002 Football throw, first. I did the discus a couple of times, first place both times. Shot put, I took second place. I could have done a lot more things, but that was enough with all the softball I am doing. Now, I wait for next year!

We need to bring God back to our United States; families with mother and dad; Ten Commandments back in schools and our daily lives; schools teaching history of our country so our children learn to be proud to live in America; parents teach respect to elders and manners to their children as they grow up. It all starts ar home. Children need to be taught that work is good and gets them what they want. This gives them confidence and self-respect. Parents cant be their kids' best friend. Tough love show the true love a parent has for their children. Teach our children how to be creative, not use their fingers on machines. Teach them how to communicate face-to-face, being able to look people in the eye and speak to them with confidence. Leave the iPhones in their pockets and talk to each other. Parents must set the example. I grew up with the saying, "Monkey see, monkey do!"

Just remember, the bigger the family the bigger rhe problems. Everyone has to work together with our Lord in the center of the family. Respect each other. As we get older as parents, put everything on paper, and make sure your children all know what is part of the estate and will All should be divided *equally no matter*

what. I thought we had the best family in the world—but it did not turn to give me more than the rest because 1 took her to South Texas and out that way. I think *money got in the way.*

I feel very good about my time with my mom. I enjoyed doing things for her and with her. She knew that also. I know she knew that if she needed something, she just had to call and I would be there for her. She had told me once she was going back to Iowa for years. Then, Bill didn't like the influence Janece and I had on her. He had other plans for her money. It is not what happens to a person that matters, it's what we become through it. I feel good about myself and doing just fine at eighty-two years of age.

Don and Janece

Just a few medals starting in 2002

Another Iowa winning team. If they buy the book, they will know where they are. I am at bottom right, second.

Lone Rock native inducted into Iowa Senior Games Hall of Fame

Don Hutchison was inducted into the Iowa Senior Games Hall of Fame on Friday, June 8.

ABOUT THE AUTHOR

Don is the second born of a family with nine boys and three girls. Family has always been important to him. He always tried to please and help his mother with housework and his father with farmwork to the best of his ability. Don did not have to be told a second time to do some things. He spent two years with the army in New Jersey at the Nike base. After discharge from the army, he went to work for American Airlines for thirty-seven years. Retirement gave him many days of freedom. He golfed for a year, bought ten acres south of Winterset, Iowa, built three ponds, a covered bridge over his overflow, a small barn, a six-bedroom house, and planted a one-acre garden. After about eight years of enjoying his adventure of that achievement, he discovered slow pitch ball. He began playing ball again, which he enjoyed so much in his youth. Remember, his family was of nine boys and three girls: a baseball team and cheerleaders. He still plays for three different teams: a seventy-five-year-old and eightyyear-old travel teams. Every June, he meets the challenges the Senior Olympics have to offer in football distance (he has taken first place in his age each year), softball accuracy, etc. He has over a hundred medals from his years of competition. In the summer of 2018, he was inducted in the Senior Games Hall of Fame. Don has been blessed in his life and enjoys sharing the good and bad of his life so far, which he knows has made him what he has become today.

www.ingramcontent.com/pod-product-compliance
Lightning Source LLC
Chambersburg PA
CBHW051539120626
46551CB00013B/1287